Useful Knots for Everyone

Useful Knots for Everyone

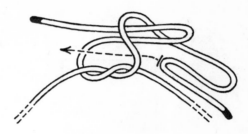

EDWARD MONTGOMERY

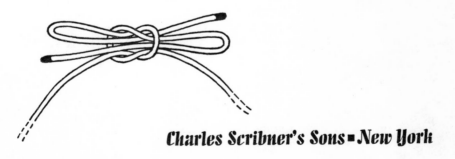

Charles Scribner's Sons ▪ New York

Copyright © 1973 Edward Poor Montgomery

Library of Congress Cataloging in Publication Data
Montgomery, Edward Poor. **Useful Knots for Everyone.** I. Knots and splices.   I.   Title. VM533.M66   640   73-2551 ISBN 0-684-13382-2 ISBN 0-684-13393-8 (pbk)

Illustrations by Charles Gottlieb based on original drawings by the Author

1 3 5 7 9 11 13 15 17 19   B/C   20 18 16 14 12 10 8 6 4 2
1 3 5 7 9 11 13 15 17 19   B/P   20 18 16 14 12 10 8 6 4 2
Printed in the United States of America

For Catherine

Contents

Introduction

Many, many books have been written on knots and their tying. Clifford W. Ashley, whose magnificent *Book of Knots* is the most comprehensive of all, lists in his bibliography one hundred and eighty-six encyclopedias, dictionaries, vocabularies, books, manuals, and monographs by British, French, Portuguese, Dutch, Swedish, German, Japanese, and American authors, dating from 1626 onward, all of which were in his personal library, and all of which deal either exclusively or partially with knots and their uses: at sea, ashore, or in various trades or handicrafts.

Why add another to the list?

I have three reasons.

The first, and certainly the most important to me, is that I wanted to write it. I wanted to write it because I expected to get a good deal of pleasure out of its planning and preparation.

Secondly, most of the books I have seen dealing with knots do so almost entirely from the point of view of the sailor. It must be admitted at once that it is to the sailor that we owe most, if not practically all, of the knots in common use. In the days of sailing ships, the safety of his ship, and often his own life depended on the security and strength of the knots, hitches, bends, splices, seizings,

12   and lashings which the sailor put into his ship's rigging, sails, running gear, hoists, tackles, and moorings. The sailor's ingenuity and inventiveness in devising ways of using rope and cord for its various purposes aboard ship was almost limitless.

But the sailor's is not the only trade or vocation, or even avocation, in which knots are regularly and frequently used. The butcher, the cook, the electrician, the farmer, the fireman, the fisherman, the gardener, the horseman, the nurse, the motorist, the weaver, the surgeon, the upholsterer and many more, all of them landlubbers, have to use knots often or occasionally. A number of these trades and occupations have developed their own knots for their own special uses, or adapted knots from others.

But perhaps the most numerous group who use knots frequently, if not regularly, seemed to me to have been overlooked almost completely by the writers of books on knots.

This group is made up of the millions of ordinary men and women who use knots about the house—in the kitchen, in the garden, on holidays or camping trips, for a great variety of purposes, from wrapping a parcel to tying up a row of tomato plants in the garden.

For most of the people in this group the books on knots and the tying of knots that I have come across seemed to me rather more unhelpful than helpful. They all try to be too comprehensive, to include too many different kinds of knots, many of them only suitable for some one specific purpose; their descriptions and drawings too complicated for the average person to understand; and their terminology and nomenclature—mostly derived from the sailor's highly technical professional vocabulary—confusing and irritating.

So it is for the ordinary man and woman *about the house* that I have written this book. I have included in it *only* those standard knots and ways of using them that seemed to me to be necessary and practical for ordinary household purposes. (There are surprisingly few.)

Above all, I wanted to keep the whole book, and particularly its descriptions and pictures of the various knots and ways of tying them, as *simple* as I possibly could. Some of the commonest knots, which, once learned, can be tied almost automatically, without thinking or even having to look at them, are difficult to describe in words, and often even more difficult to illustrate clearly. But trying to devise ways of describing and illustrating the knots *simply* was one of the pleasures—and challenges—of preparing this book.

And it was with the aim of *simplicity* that I tried to avoid using too many of the technical terms and names used by sailors, and generally adopted in most of the books on knots I have seen. As Ashley points out: "Sailors have an idiomatic language of their own which provides about everything needed for a discussion of knots." But the sailor's is a language which very few of us landlubbers have ever learned to speak. I'd make a guess that not one landsman in a hundred could give a correct definition of what the sailor means when he speaks of the "standing part" of a rope. It's quite possible too that not one sailor in fifty could give a clear definition of it *in words,* but every sailor knows exactly what it means when he uses it to describe the way to tie a knot.

So throughout the book I have tried to describe the various knots and the methods of tying them in the words that the ordinary landsman would use. In some cases that has meant adopting a terminology of my own, as the "definitions" included in the first chapter will show.

Let me give one example. I shall define that part of any length of rope or cord between the *working end* (the end in which the knot will normally be tied) and the other, or *free end,* as the *working part.* That is to say, it is the part which, when the knot or knots have been tied, will be attached *to* something, or passed *around* something, or will have some sort of pull or strain put upon it. In other words, will be doing the *work.*

Now the seaman would call that part of the length of rope either the "bight" or the "standing part," depending on whether the part is to be *active* or *inactive.* But the seaman will also use the word "bight" in a variety of other contexts. He will know what he means by it, and so will every other seaman he talks to. But it is very confusing to the *unseaman.* (The worst thing you can possibly say about practically anything done badly aboard ship is that it's "*un-*seamanlike.")

So I hereby make my apologies in advance to all deepwater and shoalwater sailors, deep-sea fishermen, yachtsmen, coastguards, and everyone else who goes to sea as a livelihood or a pastime, for taking liberties with their sacred language. But I am unrepentant. I think it's about time the landlubber was allowed his word or two in the *arcana* of knots and their tying.

Now, some explanation of how this book is planned. Chapter I is given to *definitions* of the various terms which will be used throughout the book, and some general discussion on knots and their tying.

Succeeding chapters are devoted to the various types of knots, classified according to the purposes for which they are used.

Chapter VIII is devoted to various *applications* of the knots described in earlier chapters, such as tying up parcels, trussing roasts and birds, tying up plants in the garden.

The last chapter summarizes methods of *finishing,* and it is followed by an index.

In concluding the introduction to a book it is customary to make acknowledgments to the various persons who have helped in its preparation and writing.

I have but one acknowledgment to make. It is to Mr. Clifford W. Ashley. *The Ashley Book of Knots,* published by Doubleday and Co. in 1946, is a classic of scholarship and research. Its six hundred and twenty quarto-sized pages contain descriptions and drawings of stopper knots, lanyard knots, button knots, loop knots, hitches, bends, binding knots, lashings and slings, fancy knots, splices, sinnets, and virtually every other use to which rope or cord can be put. There are no less than 3,850 numbered drawings of knots alone, and many other illustrations, all by the author. It is the most comprehensive as well as authoritative book on knots I have ever seen, or ever expect to see. My debt to him and his book is immeasurable.

Useful Knots for Everyone

Chapter i ▪ Definitions and Discussion

For the purposes of this book, a KNOT may be broadly defined as any arrangement of rope, cord, or other suitable material, which serves to fasten the rope or cord to itself, to or around another object, or to connect two or more objects. Or a KNOT may be purely decorative or ornamental. The lanyard knots, button knots, Turk's Heads, Monkey's Fists, etc., of which there are an immense variety, all fall in this category.

Some of the more common materials in which knots are tied are: hawser, rope, cord, line, string, thread, ribbon, and tape. There are of course many others.

Cordage is the generic name for all materials made up of strands of fiber tightly twisted together, of whatever composition or size.

Rope is defined as any type of large, strong cordage over three-quarters of an inch in circumference. (Rope sizes are usually given in inches of circumference—a ¾″ rope therefore is about ¼″ in diameter.) Rope includes any cordage from that minimum size up to heavy hawsers of nine or ten inches in circumference.

Line, or *cord,* is usually thought of as being thinner and lighter than rope, and is sometimes made up of strands braided together instead of twisted. (The common cotton clothesline is an example.)   19

String is thinner and lighter still, and may be made up of strands of fiber twisted together like rope, or more simply of fibers twisted together without stranding.

Thread is very thin and light, of twisted fiber, mainly used in sewing.

All the above are round in cross-section. Ribbon and tape are woven of thread and flat-like cloth, and may be of many materials: cotton, silk, linen, rayon, nylon.

Cord is the term that will be used in this book for all-round material smaller than rope or larger than thread.

The purpose of any knot, as I have defined it, is to *fasten* the rope or cord to itself, to or around another object, or to connect two or more objects.

If a knot is to do its job of fastening properly, it must fulfill three requirements: it must be capable of being *tied* easily and quickly; it must be capable of being *untied* easily and quickly; it must be capable of taking whatever strain or pull is to be put upon it without slipping, spilling, or coming loose accidentally. (That is, whatever strain is consonant with the breaking strain of the material of which it is made—you don't try to take a swordfish on a trout line.)

Now let me define the terms I will use in this book to describe the various parts of a single piece of rope or cord:

The *working end* is the last few inches of the cord which will normally be used in making the knot. A short part of the *working end* will usually protrude from the knot when it is completed.

The *working part* is all that part of the cord between the two ends.

The *free end* is the last few inches of the end of the *working part*.

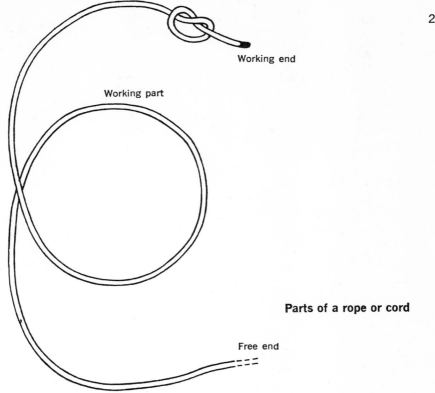

Working end

Working part

Parts of a rope or cord

Free end

(In the drawings, the *working end* is indicated by a rounded black tip on the cord. The *free end* is indicated by dotted lines, to show that the cord continues.)

(Quite often, as in tying up parcels, the *free end* is used to make the final knot which completes the job. In that case, it too becomes a *working end*.)

Every knot that can be tied consists of *open, closed,* or *crossed loops,* or *single, round,* or *two round turns* arranged in various combinations.

An *open loop* is formed when the *working end* is brought back parallel to the *working part,* but not touching it.

A *closed loop* is formed when the *working end* is brought back parallel to the *working part,* and touching it.

A *crossed loop* is formed when the *working end* is brought back across the *working part,* and touching it.

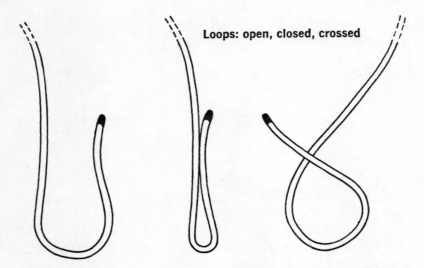

Loops: open, closed, crossed

A *single turn* is formed when the *working end* is taken *once* around either the *working part* or some other object, and brought back parallel to the *working part* and leading in the same direction.

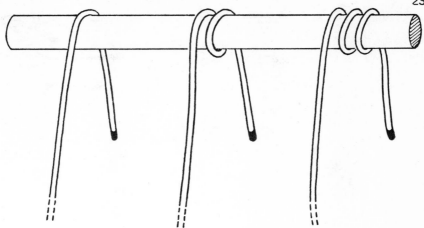

Turns: single, round, two round

A *round turn* is formed when the *working end* is taken *twice* around either the *working part* or some other object, and brought back parallel to the *working part* and leading in the same direction.

Two round turns are formed when the *working end* is taken *three times* around the *working part* or some other object, and brought back parallel to the *working part* and leading in the same direction.

The statement that every knot that can be tied consists entirely of these simple loops or turns arranged in various combinations may seem incredible to anyone looking at a complicated knot. But I think if you will take the trouble to analyze the knots in this book as you make them, you will see that the statement is true.

Sword knot

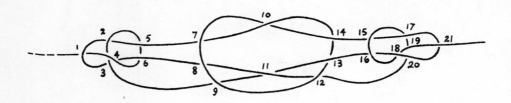

The SWORD KNOT, or OVERHAND KNOT in a SHEEPSHANK as it is sometimes called, demonstrates this point. A nicely symmetrical, highly ornamental, and totally useless knot, I can think of no useful purpose whatsoever it might serve, except as decoration. And what on earth would you decorate with it? But it must be admitted that it is, as knots go, quite intricate enough for any argument. It has, as you will see from the skeletonized drawing, no less than twenty-one separate over-and-under crossings: that is, points where one part of the cord crosses over or under another part. Very few knots have that many.

But it consists merely of four *crossed loops,* arranged as shown. To tie it, all you do is dip your right forefinger and thumb into the coil from above downward, get the forefinger under the third loop from the right, and pinch it between the forefinger and thumb. With the left thumb and forefinger pinch the third loop from

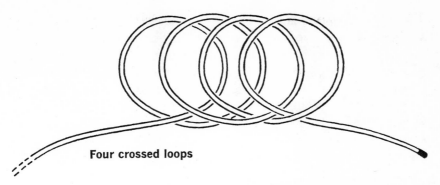

Four crossed loops

the left from below upward. Pull the loop held by the right hand to the right *over* the two loops to its right, and at the same time pull the loop held by the left hand *under* the two loops to its left, and there's your SWORD KNOT. Now to secure it, as shown in the completed knot in the drawing, thread the two ends through the right and left *closed loops.*

It is true that this is a trick knot, but it is nevertheless a true knot by any definition, and a complicated one. And it is constructed entirely from four simple loops.

It has seemed to me that it makes it easier to describe the method of tying a knot to do so in terms of the various loops or turns of which it is formed. I shall be talking of *open, closed,* and *crossed loops* and *single* and *round turns* repeatedly throughout the book.

While the word KNOT can be defined in its broadest sense to describe any of the various ways in which rope or cord or other material can be arranged as a fastening, either to itself or to something else, special words are used to describe various classes of knot, according to the purpose for which the knot is to be used.

A *binding knot* is used to join together securely the two ends of a piece of cord, whose *working part* has been passed one or more times *around* some object, as it might be a box or bundle or parcel.

A *loop knot* is made when the *working end* of the cord is fastened securely to the *working part* in such a way that a loop is formed in the *working part,* either near the *working end,* or somewhere along the length of the *working part.* The purpose of the *loop knot* is to attach the *working part* either to itself, as in tying up a parcel, or to some object like a hook, a stake, or a post, which passes through the loop.

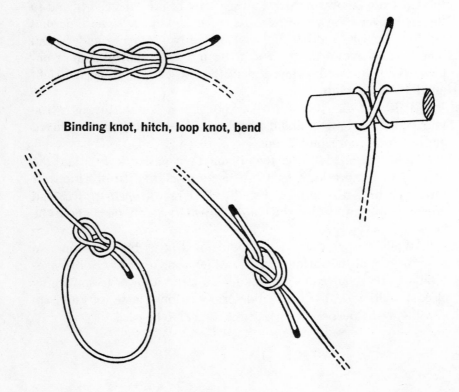

Binding knot, hitch, loop knot, bend

A *hitch* is a knot which is made either around its own *working*
part, or more commonly around another object, for the purpose of
fastening the *working part* securely to the object. In most cases the
object will be something like a post, a stake, the trunk or limb of a
tree, a log or a piece of timber.

A *bend* is a knot which securely fastens the end of one piece of
rope or cord to the end of another, separate, piece of rope or cord.
The most frequent use of a *bend* is to make one longer piece of rope
or cord out of two shorter pieces of the same size. Or a *bend* may be
used to join a piece of rope or cord to another of larger or smaller
size. Some bends are more suitable for the first purpose, others more
suitable for the second.

(In considering the definitions of *loop knots* and *hitches,* you
will have noted that the most common use of both is to fasten the
cord securely to another object. It might therefore be argued that
there is no reason to put them in separate classifications. But there is
a great difference between the two classes in the method of tying. A
loop knot is always tied "in the hand," that is, *before* it is attached
to the object, or placed around the object *after* it is tied. A *hitch,*
however, is always tied to or around the object itself. A *loop knot*
retains its shape quite independently of the object to which it may
be attached. A *hitch,* on the other hand, is entirely dependent for its
shape on the object to which it is fastened. Most *hitches* will col-
lapse completely if the object to which they are attached is
removed.)

In a number of the *binding knots, loop knots, hitches,* and
bends there is a way of tying the knot so that it may be untied simply by pulling or jerking the *working end* of the rope or cord which
protrudes from the knot. When a knot is so tied it is described as
"slipped"—a *slipped loop,* a *slipped hitch,* a *slipped bend.*

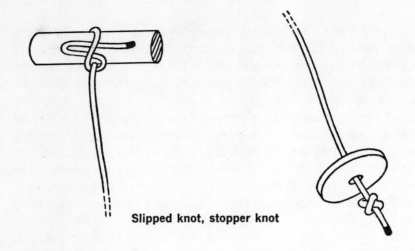

Slipped knot, stopper knot

There are several knots which may be tied in the *working end* of a rope or cord which are designed to prevent, or *"stop,"* the end from sliding through the loop or loops of another knot, or through a hole in something, like a button, a washer, or a curtain pull. They are, for this reason, called *"stopper knots."*

Some knots are named according to their classification, e.g. the OVERHAND LOOP, the ENGLISH BEND, the CLOVE HITCH. In others the word describing their classification does not appear. The SQUARE KNOT is a *binding knot;* the BOWLINE is a *loop knot;* so is the SLIPKNOT.

This question of the names of knots is a very confusing one. Often the same knot will be called by different names by the differing groups of people who use it. A sailor will hardly ever call it a SQUARE KNOT: to him it is a REEF KNOT.

Another element of confusion is that there are a number of knots, all of which are constructed and tied in the same way, but are

called by different names to distinguish the purposes for which they
are to be used. The OVERHAND KNOT, the HALF KNOT, and the
HALF HITCH are all tied exactly the same way. But the OVERHAND
KNOT is a *stopper knot;* the HALF KNOT is a *binding knot;* the HALF
HITCH is a *hitch.* The purpose of the OVERHAND KNOT is to prevent
(*"stop"*) the cord from slipping through something; the purpose of
the HALF KNOT is to secure the cord *around* something; the purpose
of the HALF HITCH is to secure the cord *to* something. The OVER-
HAND KNOT is always tied and drawn up *in the cord itself.* The
HALF KNOT is tied when the *working part* of the cord has been
passed *around* something, and the *working end* comes out of the
knot in the opposite direction from the *working part,* and in line
with it. The HALF HITCH is also tied when the *working part* has
been passed around something, but the *working end* comes out of
the knot more or less at right angles to the *working part.*

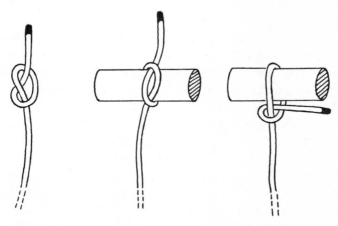

Overhand knot, half knot, half hitch

Now for a few minor definitions of words that will be constantly used in the following pages.

A knot is said to be *"spilled"* when it comes loose or untied when a strain is put upon the *working part* of the rope or cord.

A knot that has been pulled up so tight by a strong strain that it becomes impossible or very difficult to untie is said to be *"jammed."* There are some knots that are deliberately so tied that they *"jam"* when pulled up tight. They are called *"jam knots."*

The *"lead"* is the direction in which any part of the rope or cord leads from the knot when completed.

A *"stopping"* is a temporary method of preventing the cut end of a rope from fraying.

A *"whipping"* is a permanent method of preventing the cut end of a rope or cord from fraying, and consists of a number of turns of material much smaller than the rope or cord—fine twine or thread —wound tightly around the end and secured so that the turns will not slip off.

A *"seizing"* is a method of preventing two parallel parts of a rope or cord from sliding on each other, and consists of a number of turns of material smaller than the rope or cord, wound tightly around the two parts, and secured so that the parts will not slide or slip.

To *"middle"* a piece of rope or cord is to bring the two ends together to form a *closed loop*. The end of the loop is the middle of the rope or cord.

To *"marry"* two pieces of rope or cord, or two parts of the same piece, is to bring the parts together, parallel to each other, and touching.

The only tools that are needed to *tie* the knots described in this book are the normal manual complement of two thumbs and eight

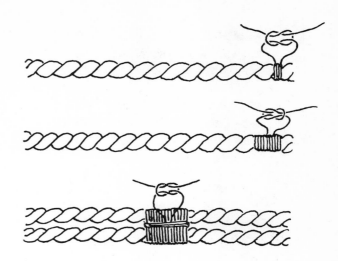

Stopping, whipping, seizing

fingers, plus a sharp knife or scissors to cut the material to the desired length.

There are, however, several tools that are useful in *untying*
knots, especially if the knots have been pulled up very tight under
strong strain.

To work loose the parts of a knot so that it can be untied easily
the sailor uses a *marlingspike*. But since this is designed for working
with rope, it is too big and clumsy for use on the much smaller-sized
cord or string found in the household. However, almost any round,
pointed short length of metal or wood will serve as a marlingspike
for ordinary use. Best of all, perhaps, would be the kind of steel
pricker with a wooden handle such as is used for making holes in
cloth for some kinds of embroidery. But half a fair-sized steel or

wooden knitting needle will do almost as well, or for thin string a meat skewer or an ordinary orange-wood stick for cleaning the finger nails. One caution: if the point is very sharp it's wise to file it or grind it down so that it is blunt enough not to cause a jabbed finger or palm if the tool should slip.

Not so essential, but very useful is a small pair of needle-nosed pliers for gripping the knot firmly while working it loose. Indeed, with the pliers closed, the nose itself will make a good marlingspike in cord that it is not too thin. In the book, to avoid confusion, I will refer to whatever serves as a substitute marlingspike as a *"pricker."*

While we're on the subject of *untying* knots, there's one general piece of advice I'd like to give. When you have to untie a knot, don't just pick at it aimlessly, hoping that eventually something will give enough so that you can loosen the knot. Look at the knot closely to see how the various loops have been combined. Find the *working end* which protrudes from the knot. Locate the loop in the knot nearest to it. Then work the end back through the loop, until the loop comes free. Continue pushing the end back through the succeeding loops, until the whole knot has been loosened and you can untie it easily. Sometimes it may be easier to start with the *working part* rather than the *working end,* and push that back through the loops. I think you'll find approaching the knot this way will save you a lot of time, bad temper, and maybe a broken fingernail or two.

Before moving on to detailed descriptions of the various *binding knots, loop knots, hitches,* and *bends,* there is one overall caution which applies to almost every knot that can be tied. When a knot is tightened securely it is said to be *"drawn up,"* and this expression will be used throughout the book to describe the tightening process.

Very few knots can be drawn up really securely merely by pulling on the parts of the rope or cord which protrude from the knot. As well as pulling or jerking, one must work the knot into its correct shape with the fingers. Your must start by pulling the knot loosely together by the *working end* and the *working part,* then work it tighter between the fingers and thumbs, then pull again, and go on repeating the two operations until a final pull brings the knot up snug and secure and in the right shape. Only in this way can most knots be made truly secure so that they will hold without danger of slipping or spilling.

One other piece of advice. The tying of knots does not come naturally, like eating or watching TV or falling downstairs. Tying knots, like playing the guitar, driving a car, or hammering a nail without hammering your thumb, requires practice. You will find that even the simple standard knots described in this book will require at least some practice before you learn how to tie them quickly, easily, and without having to think what you are doing. Get yourself a short length—seven or eight feet will be plenty—of the white braided nylon cord about an eighth of an inch in diameter which is now sold almost everywhere for curtain pulls or blind cord. It is very suitable for practicing, as it is fairly supple and yet holds the shape of the knot well so you can see its construction clearly. It is also rather slippery, which makes it easy to untie the knot you are practicing. Then, as you go through this book, take your piece of nylon cord and make each knot several times until you feel familiar with it. In the process you will also learn how you can untie each knot most easily and quickly—remembering always that it is just as important to be able to *untie* knots as it is to be able to *tie* them.

Chapter ii ▪ The Basic Knots

In Chapter I I emphasised that virtually all knots—and certainly all described in this book—consist of *open, closed,* or *crossed loops,* or *single* or *round turns,* arranged in various combinations.

In this chapter I will describe the simplest combinations. These are the basic knots, which will reappear again and again in the following chapters, either by themselves, or in combination with another basic knot, but more often as the initial stage in a more complex knot.

The OVERHAND KNOT

This is the most elementary knot of all. To tie it you make a *crossed loop,* then bring the *working end* over and around the *working* part, pass it through the loop, and draw up tight.

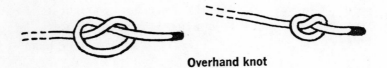

Overhand knot

But just because it is simple doesn't mean that it isn't useful,
for two purposes. The first is to prevent the *working end* of the cord
from fraying when the cord is too thin to put on a *stopping*. The
second, and more important, is as a *stopper knot,* to prevent the
working end from slipping back through the adjacent loop of a
more complicated knot and so allowing the knot to come loose or
spill, or to *stop* the *working end* from sliding back through, say, a
button, or washer, or piece of cloth.

The OVERHAND KNOT DOUBLED

This is tied exactly the same way as the single OVERHAND KNOT, except the *working end* is passed *twice* around the *working part* before
being passed through the loop. Oddly, though it looks rather clumsy
and misshapen when it is loose, it draws up into a neat and symmetrical shape when completed. It is a bit more bulky than its single
parent, and therefore that much more useful as a *stopper knot.* Most
women who do a lot of sewing have learned to make both the OVER-
HAND KNOT and OVERHAND KNOT DOUBLED single-handed. They
moisten the tip of the right forefinger and thumb, and make a loose
round turn around the tip of the right forefinger. Then they roll the
crossing of the turn between the forefinger and the ball of the thumb
into the loop, forming the OVERHAND KNOT. When made in this
way, they are known as THUMB KNOTS.

Overhand knot doubled

The HALF KNOT

This is exactly the same knot as the OVERHAND KNOT, and is tied in the same way. But it is called by a different name because it serves a quite different purpose. The OVERHAND KNOT is always tied and drawn up in the cord itself. The HALF KNOT is always tied *around* something, either the *working part* of the cord, or another cord, or around a parcel or bundle. In the latter case it is usually tied as the start of one or another of the *binding knots,* notably the SQUARE KNOT (see p. 42) and the BOWKNOT (see p. 47). By itself it is obviously completely insecure.

The HALF KNOT and its sister, the HALF HITCH, are the two basic knots used in making that decorative knot-work which the sailor calls *square-knotting* and the landsman (or landswoman) calls *macramé.* The HALF KNOT or HALF HITCH is tied around one or two strands of similar cord. When a HALF KNOT is tied, it is usual to follow it with another HALF KNOT, but reversed, producing a SQUARE KNOT—hence the sailor's name *square-knotting.* A variety of handsome patterns can be produced with just these two simple knots arranged in different combinations.

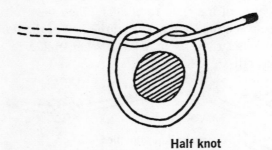

Half knot

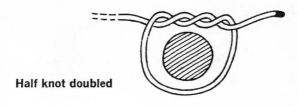

Half knot doubled

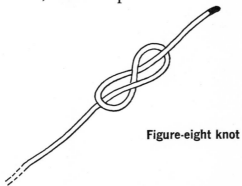

The HALF KNOT DOUBLED

This again is the same knot as the OVERHAND KNOT DOUBLED, tied the same way. But like the HALF KNOT, it always tied around something else enclosed in the loop. It is the start of the SQUARE KNOT DOUBLED (see p. 46).

The FIGURE-EIGHT KNOT

To tie this, make a *crossed loop* with the *working end* by leading it back to the left over the *working part*. Pass the *working end* around and under the *working part* and pass it through the *crossed loop* from front to back, and draw up.

Figure-eight knot

This can be used as a *stopper knot,* like the OVERHAND KNOT DOUBLED. But it does not draw up into quite such a neat shape. The entwined crossed loops, which give it its figure-8 appearance, make it nicely symmetrical when loose. But it is mainly decorative rather than useful. I include it here because it is the basis for one of the commoner *loop knots* (see p. 57).

The CROSSING KNOT

This can hardly be described as a knot at all. It merely serves to hold two pieces of cord together where they cross at right angles to each other. But it is indispensable in tying up parcels securely, and

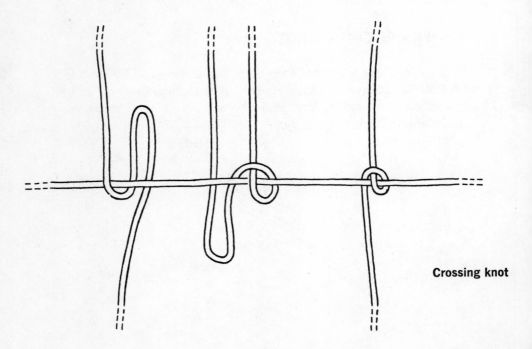

Crossing knot

is used so often for that purpose that it must have its place among the basic knots.

Imagine you have taken a turn around the sides of a parcel and secured the cord with a knot. Then you lead the cord away from the knot at right angles to the first turn, so that you can take a turn around the ends of the parcel. The cord will then pass over the first turn on the opposite side of the parcel from the knot, and you want to hold the two parts of the cord together.

Take the cord *over* the part it is crossing, make a *closed loop* in it, and pass the loop upward *under* the crossing cord to the right, and pull it upward to put a slight strain on the crossing cord. Then bring the loop over its own part of the cord and to the left, then downward *under* the crossing cord. Now by drawing the loop open you can pull the whole working length of the cord through. Doing it this way, with a loop, is much quicker than hunting for the *free end* and making the knot with it instead of the loop.

The HALF HITCH

The HALF HITCH is identical in construction with the OVERHAND KNOT and the HALF KNOT. The *working end* is passed through a *crossed loop* in the *working part* in the same way. Like the HALF KNOT, the HALF HITCH is always tied *around* something, its own *working part,* another piece of cord, a ring, a stake, a post, the limb of a tree.

But it takes a different shape from the HALF KNOT when completed, and is used for a different purpose, hence the difference in names. Whereas in the HALF KNOT the *working end* and the *working part* come out of the knot leading in opposite directions and in

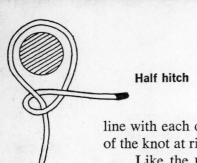

Half hitch

line with each other, in the HALF HITCH the *working end* comes out of the knot at right angles to the *working part*.

Like the HALF KNOT, the HALF HITCH is not at all secure by itself. But it is constantly used in tying up parcels, for securing knots that would otherwise slip, as the start of other *hitches* or combinations of them, and for a variety of other purposes. Like the previous knots, it will reappear often in the following pages.

The HAMMOCK HITCH

This variant of the HALF KNOT is most useful in tying up parcels, especially those that are long and narrow, say, for example, a rolled-up rug or bolt of cloth.

Your cord has already been secured near one end of the roll. Take the *working part* leading from the knot that has been made and, holding it in the left hand, make a right-angled elbow in the cord and pass a *single* turn around the roll with the *working end*. Take the *working end* over the *working part,* and pass it under the elbow to the right, and draw up taut against the elbow.

This was the sailor's classical method of lashing up his hammock for stowing when he had been shaken out of it to go on watch or to start the morning's routine of sanding, scrubbing, and holystoning the decks. "Seven turns," no more, no less; that is, seven hitches from head to foot of the rolled-up hammock. And woe betide the apprentice seaman who put on one hitch too many or too few. He had to learn, too, that there is a right way and a wrong way to pass the HAMMOCK HITCH. The right way is as described above, with the *working end* taken over the *working part* and under the elbow.

The wrong way is to pass the *working end* under the *working part* and up over the elbow. Done the wrong way, the HAMMOCK HITCH will not be as firm, nor hold the tension in the cord as well. When you make the HAMMOCK HITCH the wrong way what you are in fact doing is to tie a series of HALF HITCHES around the object. When you make the HAMMOCK HITCH the right way you are tying a series of HALF KNOTS around the object.

Get a mailing tube or something similar—a piece of rolled-up newspaper will do. Make a series of HAMMOCK HITCHES around it the *wrong* way. Slide the hitches off one end. They will spill completely, and you'll be left with just a straight piece of cord. Now make the HAMMOCK HITCH the *right* way, and slide off the end. Pull the two ends of cord, and you will find that the HALF KNOTS become a series of OVERHAND KNOTS, thus demonstrating why the wrong way it not as firm and does not hold the tension in the cord as well as the right way.

At sea this is called a MARLINE HITCH. But I think the name HAMMOCK HITCH is both more descriptive and easier to remember.

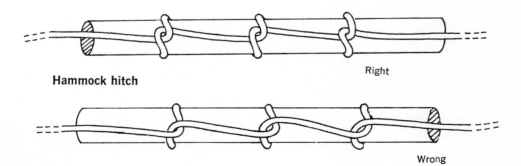

Hammock hitch

Right

Wrong

Chapter iii ▪ The Binding Knots

A *binding knot* is used to join together securely the two ends of a piece of cord, whose *working part* has been passed one or more times *around* some object, as it might be a box or bundle or parcel.

The SQUARE KNOT

This is one of the simplest, easiest, and most commonly used of the *binding knots.* As with most of them, there are really two *working ends* in the same length of cord, as the *working part* has already been passed around the parcel or bundle or whatever it encloses.

It is started by tying a HALF KNOT, drawing up the two ends so that the *working part* is snug around the bundle after the knot is made.

Now tie another HALF KNOT on top of the first, but in reverse, in such a way that each end comes out alongside its own *working* part, and *on the same side* of the loop through which they both pass. Left loose, the knot appears as two *closed loops* leading in opposite directions and linked together, the *working end* and *working part* of

Square knot

one loop coming out *over* the opposing loop, the *working end* and *working part* of the other loop coming out *under* its opposite.

The great advantage of the SQUARE KNOT is that it is extremely easy to untie. Unless it has been unnecessarily tightly drawn up, you can spill a SQUARE KNOT simply by pulling or tugging on one or the other of the *working ends*. As you pull on the end, you bring it around so that its loop straightens out and the end is leading in the same direction as its own *working part*. The other loop then collapses into a RING HITCH (see p. 77) which will slide along the end that has been pulled, and off it to free both ends completely.

And that brings us to the great weakness of the SQUARE KNOT, a weakness that can become positively dangerous if the knot is used for the wrong purpose.

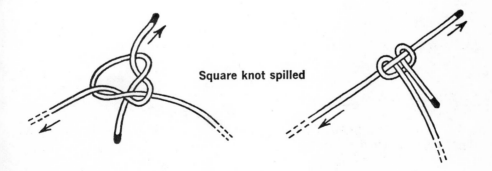

Square knot spilled

The SQUARE KNOT *must never be used* to fasten (or *"bend"*) one length of rope or cord to another length. If it is so used, say to make one long length of rope out of two short lengths, and the rope accidentally brushes against something or is pulled around something, one of the *working ends* may catch or snag, with the same result as if the end were deliberately jerked or pulled. The knot will spill, and the two lengths of rope come apart.

Used as a *bend,* the SQUARE KNOT can become actually murderous if it is made to take the strain of hoisting a heavy weight or a man. Ashley says: *"There have probably been more lives lost as a result of using a SQUARE KNOT as a bend (to tie two ropes together) than from the failure of any other half-dozen knots combined."*

There are two ways in which the SQUARE KNOT can be made more secure against the risk of accidental spilling (though, let me emphasize, neither of them could *ever* justify its use as a *bend*).

The SQUARE KNOT SECURED (A)

Draw the knot up snug, and then make a HALF HITCH with each of the *working ends* around the *working part* next to it, and pull the hitches up tight against the loops of the knot.

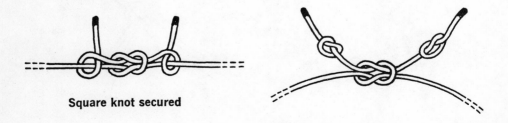

Square knot secured

Tie OVERHAND KNOTS in both *working ends* as close up to the knot as possible.

This may be just a shade more secure than the first method, but it makes a very ugly and bulky knot, and completely spoils the neatness and symmetry of the plain SQUARE KNOT. I prefer the first method.

Now let's go back for a moment to the point where you have started your SQUARE KNOT by tying the first HALF KNOT. What happens if you tie the second HALF KNOT, not in reverse, but in the same way as the first? Then you will find each *working end* and its own *working part* coming out of the loops not on the same side but on opposite sides, so that the loop crosses between them.

And what you have done is to make yourself the much-despised GRANNY KNOT, and if unluckily a sailor should see you doing it, you'll hear rude noises.

The GRANNY KNOT

Actually there is not all that much reason to despise the GRANNY KNOT. It is a perfectly good *binding knot* in itself, and though certainly nothing like as secure as the SQUARE KNOT, once drawn up it

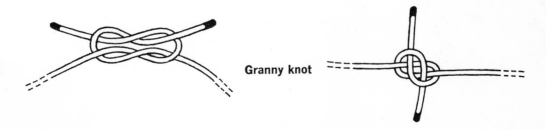

Granny knot

will take a strain quite tolerably well without slipping. What's wrong with it is that once drawn up tight, it tends to *jam,* and is next to impossible to untie without using a *pricker* to pry it loose. And compared with the neat and symmetrical SQUARE KNOT, it looks simply hideous, the *working ends* and the *working parts* all coming out of the knot every which way.

The SQUARE KNOT DOUBLED

This is a useful variation if you have to tie up something slippery, like, say, a rolled roast of beef, or a bundle of clothes that tends to expand when you've tightened the *working part* around it. One trouble with the SQUARE KNOT is that it can be difficult to keep up the tension on the *working part* with the first HALF KNOT while you are tying the second, because the first HALF KNOT tends to slip unless it is held down. That does not matter if a willing husband or wife is around to hold it in place with a forefinger, while the knotter ties the second HALF KNOT. But such help is not always available.

In that case, make a HALF KNOT DOUBLED (see p. 37) by taking two turns of the *working ends* around each other instead of only one. Now when you draw the *working part* up tight around the roast or bundle, the HALF KNOT DOUBLED will hold against the tension in

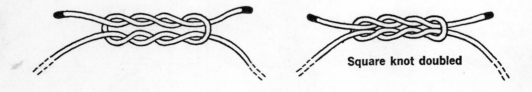

Square knot doubled

the cord while you make another HALF KNOT DOUBLED on top of
the first, and draw the completed knot up tight.

This is rather a clumsy-looking knot when finished. But it is very effective, and particularly useful in the kitchen.

The BOWKNOT

The BOWKNOT is really only a more decorative way of tying the SQUARE KNOT.

As with the SQUARE KNOT, begin by tying a HALF KNOT. With the left hand, make a *closed loop* in the *working end* which leads to the left, and lead the loop to the right. Hold the loop between the left forefinger and thumb, with the thumb resting on the HALF KNOT

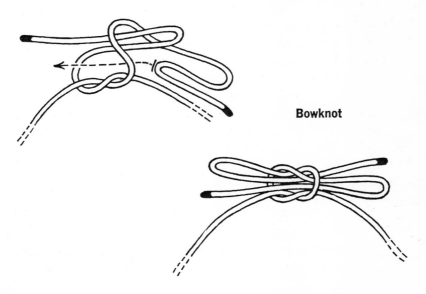

Bowknot

48 and holding it down, if necessary. With the *working end* leading to the right, with the right hand take a *single turn* around the tip of the left thumb, and push a *closed loop* through the turn, withdrawing your left thumb as you push the loop through the turn. Catch the loop between the left thumb and forefinger, at the same time taking the loop they have been holding between the right thumb and forefinger. Now you draw the knot up by pulling on both loops at the same time, evening up the lengths of the loops and *working ends* if necessary to make the knot neat.

Thus, when the BOWKNOT is completed and drawn up, you can see that its construction is identical with that of the SQUARE KNOT, except that in the BOWKNOT you have a *working end* and a loop coming out of the knot on either side, instead of the *working ends* only, as in the SQUARE KNOT.

Most people can tie a BOWKNOT automatically, without having to think about it, largely, I suppose, because it is the first knot a child has to learn in order to be able to tie his or her shoelaces. And strangely enough, most people instinctively tie it correctly, which they don't do with a SQUARE KNOT. (I've been tying knots now for a good many more than fifty years, but I still occasionally make a GRANNY KNOT if I'm not paying attention.) Now it's perfectly possible to tie a GRANNY BOWKNOT. Try it sometime and see. But people hardly ever do. Odd, isn't it?

The BOWKNOT is, of course, beautifully easy to untie. Just pull on one or both of the *working ends,* and the whole knot spills instantly. And just because of that, it is damnably and often annoyingly insecure, as everyone knows who has had a shoelace come untied when he was running to catch a bus. There are two ways in which to make a BOWKNOT more secure, neither of which is completely spill-proof, but is at least an improvement.

The BOWKNOT SECURED (A)

When you reach the point in tying your BOWKNOT that you are holding the loop in the *working end* between your left thumb and forefinger with the thumb resting on the HALF KNOT, instead of taking a *single turn* around the tip of your thumb with the *working end* leading to the right, take a full *round turn.* Push the loop in that *working end* through the *round turn* as you did with the *single turn,* and draw the knot up as before. This is, I think, by far the neatest way to secure the BOWKNOT.

The BOWKNOT SECURED (B)

This is perhaps a simpler and quicker way than the one above, but is bulkier and not so neat.

Simply take the two loops projecting from each side of the knot and with them tie a HALF KNOT over the middle of the BOWKNOT.

As I have said, neither of these ways is wholly reliable, but they are considerably more so than the BOWKNOT unsecured at all.

The BAG KNOT

This is a knot that I never knew about until just a few years ago, and one that I don't think is in very common use. At least I have never seen it used, except by me. I have called it the BAG KNOT because its principal use is to secure the neck of a bag or sack tightly and permanently to keep any of its contents from spilling or leaking even under severe man-handling. But I have found it an incredibly versatile little knot, which serves a wide variety of purposes around the house.

It is a deceptively simple knot to look at, but the tying of it is not easy to explain in words, or even in a diagram.

There are two ways to tie it. The first way described below must be used when the BAG KNOT is to be tied around an object some distance from either of its ends.

Drop a few inches of the *working end* over the object from front to back and bring it around underneath to the right of the *working part* and over the object again from front to back leading to the left, so that it forms a *crossed loop* around the object in the *working part*. With the left hand pull up an *open loop* in the *work-ing part*. With the right hand pass the *working end* from front to back to the right of the *working part* and then upward under the

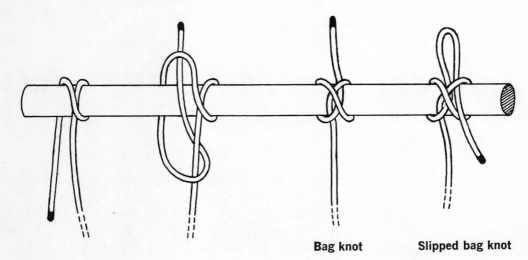

Bag knot   **Slipped bag knot**

working part and through the loop. Both the *working end* and the
working part should emerge from between the two outer turns of
the knot, and leading in opposite directions. Now pull on both the
working end and the *working part* simultaneously to draw the knot
up, which should be as tightly as possible.

If you are tying the BAG KNOT close to the end of an object, as
it might be the cut end of a rope on which you want to put a *stopping* to prevent the rope from fraying, or the neck of a well-filled
bag, or a bundle of garden stakes, there's a neat quick trick way of
tying it.

You can amuse yourself practicing it on your left thumb,
which is probably the handiest "object" you can use for practicing a
number of knots, including several of the *hitches*. The drawings
show it tied over the thumb.

Drop a few inches of the *working end* over the thumb, leading
a little to the left. Bring it around to the left of the *working part* and
over the thumb leading to the right, so that it forms a *crossed loop*
in the *working part* around the thumb. If necessary, catch the *working end* between the middle and ring fingers of the left hand. With
the thumb and forefinger of the right hand pull the loop in the *working part* upward a couple of inches to form an *open loop,* give it a
half-twist *counterclockwise* to make a *crossed loop,* drop the loop
over the tip of the thumb, and bring it back to the left over the
HALF KNOT that has been formed around the thumb in the *working
part*. With the right hand pull alternately on the *working end* and
working part to draw the knot up.

In either case, when you come to cut the cord to trim the completed knot, leave a good inch or more of both the *working end* and
the *working part* protruding from the knot. If for neatness' sake you
want to trim the ends shorter than that, as you would if you were

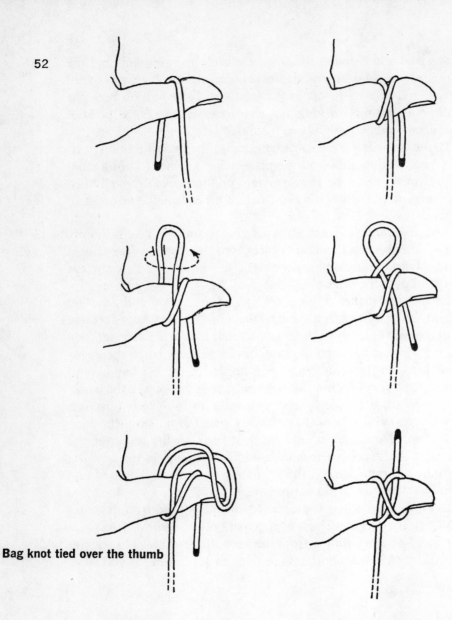

Bag knot tied over the thumb

using the BAG KNOT for *stopping* the cut end of a rope, it is best to tie another HALF KNOT over the BAG KNOT.

If you will study the knot after it is made, or look closely at the diagram, you will see that the BAG KNOT is indeed simple. All it is is a HALF KNOT with a *round turn* over it, which when the knot is tightly drawn up, brings pressure to bear on the HALF KNOT to hold it securely against slipping.

The great virtue of the BAG KNOT is that once tied tightly around something soft, like the neck of a cloth bag or sack, a roll of paper, or even around a bundle of stakes or sticks, it will hold forever and maintain its tension. However, whatever it is tied around must be fairly small in diameter—not more than three or four inches or so—because when tied around anything larger, the HALF KNOT becomes so elongated that the *round turn* over it will not keep it secure.

To demonstrate how secure it is when properly used, I have even used it to attach a nozzle to a garden hose when I was lacking a proper hose clamp. In that case I used a longish piece of strong cord, made the BAG KNOT around the hose after inserting the nozzle, and hitched both ends of the cord to a couple of lengths of wood. I stood on one piece of wood, and hauled up on the other with my hands until the knot was drawn up extra tight. Even after six months of use the BAG KNOT was still holding, and never a sign of a leak at the joint between hose and nozzle.

But every advantage has its disadvantage. The BAG KNOT is *so* secure that it is almost impossible to untie without using a *pricker*. I would defy even Alexander the Great to untie it without cutting it, as he had to do with the Gordian Knot, unless his sword was small enough to be used as a marlingspike, by "slipping" it, as described below.

However, this disadvantage is very easily overcome, without impairing the security of the knot at all.

(Ashley usually refers to this knot as "CONSTRICTOR KNOT." He believes he may have invented it, and I cannot doubt his claim, for I have never seen it referred to or described in any other book of knots. But somehow the word "constrictor," although descriptively accurate, seems a little sesquipedalian to me. Ashley himself lists it among several other knots which he calls BAG KNOTS, whose principal use is to secure the necks of bags or sacks. As BAG KNOT seems to me so much simpler and easier to remember, I have taken the liberty of re-christening his invention.)

While on this subject, if you have to put a binding knot on any sort of soft bundle, say of clothing or laundry, which is too large to be secured with a BAG KNOT, you can achieve almost the same security very simply. Make a FIGURE-EIGHT KNOT near the *working end* of your piece of cord or string. Pass the cord around the bundle and thread the *working part* through the upper loop in the FIGURE-EIGHT, i.e. nearest the *working end*. Holding the *working end* with the left hand, with your right hand draw up on the *working part* away from you, sliding the FIGURE-EIGHT along it. When you have got the cord around the bundle as tight as you want it, hold the *working end* and the *working part* opposite it firmly with the left thumb and forefinger to keep the FIGURE-EIGHT from slipping, and with the right hand make a HALF HITCH with the *working part* around the *working part* below the FIGURE-EIGHT on the side toward you. Draw up very tightly on both the *working end* and the *working part* to secure the FIGURE-EIGHT and the HALF HITCH. Then trim the *working part* coming out of the HALF HITCH to equal the *working end* coming out of the FIGURE-EIGHT.

The SLIPPED BAG KNOT

You will need to use a few more inches of the *working end* for this, so that when you reach the stage of passing the *working end* upward underneath the turns, you can double the *working end* back on itself to form a *closed loop,* and pass the loop upward underneath the turns, leaving the *working end* protruding from the knot in the same direction as the *working part.* Draw up the knot tightly as before, cut the *working part* an inch or so from the knot, and trim the *working end* to match. Now a pull or a jerk will spill the HALF KNOT from under the *round turn,* and the knot will come free.

This is a useful version for the kitchen, to tie those polyethylene bags which have become so deservedly popular with housewives in recent years for storing salads and vegetables and other things in the refrigerator.

Chapter iv ▪The Loop Knots

A *loop knot* is made when the *working end* of the cord is fastened securely to the *working part* in such a way that a loop is formed in the *working part,* either near the *working end,* or somewhere along the length of the *working part.* The purpose of the *loop knot* is to attach the *working part* either to itself, as in tying up a parcel, or to some object like a hook, a stake, or post which passes through the loop.

The OVERHAND LOOP

The OVERHAND LOOP is the simplest and easiest to tie of all the *loop knots.* Take the *working end* and bring it back alongside the *working part* to form a *closed loop* of a little more than the length desired. Then make an OVERHAND KNOT with the loop and draw up.

Though it is quickly tied, its disadvantage is that if a strong strain is put upon it, it tends to jam badly, and may need to be opened up with a *pricker* before it can be untied. Also, once a strain has been put upon it, the loop tends to stay closed, making it awkward to pass the *working part,* or another cord or object, through the loop a second time if needed.

Overhand loop

and figure eight loop

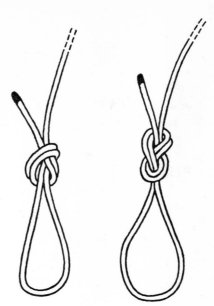

The FIGURE-EIGHT LOOP

Double back the *working end* against the working part to form a closed loop of a little more than the length desired. Then tie a FIGURE-EIGHT KNOT with the doubled cord, by bringing the loop back and over the doubled cord to the left, around and under and back to the right through the *crossed loop* made in the doubled cord. Draw up tightly.

    This loop is particularly useful to the angler who is fishing with monofilament spinning line. Monofilament is tricky, slippery, rigid stuff that does not take kindly to having knots tied in it. Many of the knots which are completely secure tied in any other material, tend to slip when tied in monofilament. A loop made in monofilament with a FIGURE-EIGHT knot and tightly drawn up is less liable to slip than most.

But don't expect to be able to untie it easily, whatever type of cord or line you make it in. It jams under strain even more thoroughly than the OVERHAND LOOP.

The SLIPKNOT

The SLIPKNOT is really a running NOOSE, although it can be secured to make it a non-slip *loop knot*.

It can be tied in two different ways, each suitable for differing purposes.

The first variation, and the most usual, is made by tying a

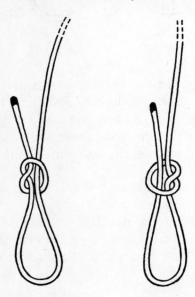

Slipknot and slipknot reversed

HALF KNOT with the *working end* around the *working part,* and
drawing it up. Now the loop can be made either larger or smaller as
desired merely by sliding the HALF KNOT along the *working part* in
either direction.

The SLIPKNOT REVERSED

Or the SLIPKNOT can be made in reverse by tying a HALF KNOT in
the *working part* and threading the *working end* through the HALF
KNOT to form the loop before drawing up. Now it is the *working
end* that slides through the HALF KNOT to make the loop larger or
smaller.

Suppose that having got your loop to the size you need, you
want to secure it to prevent any further slipping in either direction.

The SLIPKNOT SECURED (A)

In the first version you simply make a HALF HITCH with the *working part* around the *working end.*

The SLIPKNOT SECURED (B)

In the second version, the SLIPKNOT REVERSED, the HALF HITCH is
made with the *working end* around the *working part.* This version
can also be secured (but only in one direction) by making an OVER-
HAND KNOT in the *working end* close up to the HALF KNOT when
you have adjusted the loop to the desired size.

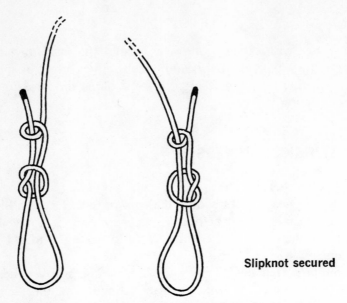

Slipknot secured

As is obvious from their appearance, neither of the versions of the SLIPKNOT, even when secured with a HALF HITCH, is a very strong or reliable knot. But they are so simply tied and untied that they are useful for doing up a parcel or bundle temporarily where more secure knots are not needed. The second version, without the HALF HITCH, is also useful as a temporary *stopper knot,* because it can be spilled instantly by simply pulling on the *working end.*

The BOWLINE

Now here is the queen of the *loop knots,* if not of all the knots that man has ever devised. It is certainly the most frequently used of the *loop knots* aboard ship, whether sail, steam, motor, or—one must

add nowadays—nuclear reactor. It is easy to tie, once you have the
trick of it; easy to untie, unless the rope or cord in which it is made
has been badly soaked as well as strained; exceptionally strong and
secure and proof against slipping; and, because of the construction
of the knot itself, the loop tends to stay open even after a heavy
strain has been put upon it.

The way the sailor ties it sounds rather complicated when described in words, but once thoroughly learned, it will become completely automatic, so that you will be able to tie it without thinking,
without looking, in the dark or blindfolded.

I'll try to make it as simple as I can.

Take the *working part* of the cord in the left hand, and the
working end in the right hand, with the palms of both hands down,
and bring the hands together so that an *open loop* of the right size is
formed with both the *working end* and the *working part* leading
away from you. Lay the right forefinger along the *working end,* and
with it lay the *working end* over the *working part,* so that you have
formed a large *crossed loop*. Now push the *working part* forward a
little with the left hand and at the same time bear down a little with
the right forefinger on the *working end*. As you do this turn both
hands over and outward, so that the palms of both are upward. This
motion forms a second, smaller *crossed loop* in the *working part,*
with the *working end* protruding through the loop, from underneath
upward.

Now with the forefinger and thumb of the left hand nip the
smaller *crossed loop* at the crossing and hold the loop steady and
open. With the right hand pass the *working end* around behind the
working part from right to left, and thread the *working end* down
through the smaller *crossed loop,* parallel to and alongside the part
of the *working end* already contained in the loop.

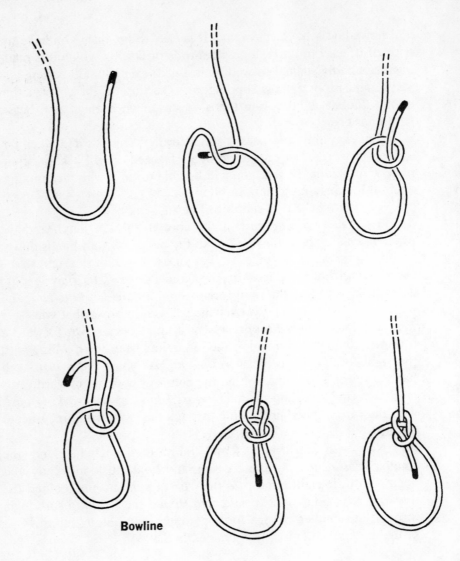

Bowline

In drawing up the BOWLINE you must use both hands evenly,
the left hand pulling on the *working end* and the part alongside it,
the right hand tightening the knot by simultaneously pulling on the
working part where it comes out of the top of the knot.

If you will look at the finished knot in the diagram, and analyze it in terms of the knots already described, you will see that the
BOWLINE is really a HALF HITCH taken around a *closed loop,* with
the *working part* in which the HALF HITCH is made threaded
through the *closed loop* beyond the HALF HITCH.

And you *could* tie a BOWLINE by making it just that way, but
you would find that you would have to thread the whole length of
the *working part* through the *closed loop* to do it. And if you were
trying to tie a BOWLINE in the end of a hundred-fathom length of
nine-inch hawser, that might become a little tedious.

Sorry if I haven't made it sound as simple as I would like to,
but I think if you will study the diagram carefully, and then practice
a few times with your bit of nylon cord, you'll find yourself tying the
BOWLINE as quickly and neatly as any sailor.

The great virtue of the BOWLINE is that most of the strain is
taken by the HALF HITCH, and not much by the *closed loop* which
forms the other part. The loop therefore usually remains a little
loose, so that when you come to untying the BOWLINE all you have
to do is to push the *working part* outside the knot backward through
the *closed loop* to loosen the HALF HITCH, and the whole knot
comes apart easily. A properly tied BOWLINE should never jam, and
never need a marlingspike or a *pricker* to work it loose.

Slipped bowline

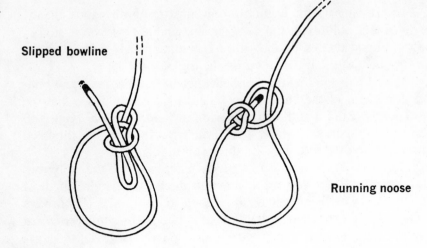

Running noose

The SLIPPED BOWLINE

The straight BOWLINE is, as I have said, quite easy to untie, but it can, if desirable, be made still easier by converting it into a *slipped knot.*

When you have reached the stage of getting the *working end,* which is lying inside the smaller *crossed loop,* around and in back of the *working part,* draw out a little more of the *working end,* double it back on itself to make a *closed loop,* and then pass this *closed loop* back of the *working part* and down through the *crossed loop* as you did with the single *working end,* and draw up the knot as before.

Now you will have some of the *working end* protruding from the knot, leading in the same direction as the *working part.* To untie the knot, then, all you have to do is to work it a little loose, and pull on the *working end*. The loop will slide through the HALF HITCH, and the knot will spill.

This is useful when you are using the BOWLINE to tie up a bundle or package that you—or someone else—may want to untie quickly and easily. It is just as secure as the straight BOWLINE and just as quickly tied.

The RUNNING NOOSE

Any of the *loop knots* above can be converted into a RUNNING NOOSE simply by threading the *working part* through the *loop knot* to form a larger loop.

The ENGLISH LOOP

The foregoing *loop knots* have all been made with the *working end* by securing it to the *working part*. It may sometimes be necessary to make a *loop knot,* or a series of *loop knots,* either in the middle of the cord, or spaced out along its length. This, and the succeeding knots, are examples.

The construction of the ENGLISH LOOP is identical with the ENGLISH BEND (see p. 83), and starts out the same way as the SLIPKNOT REVERSED (see p. 59). Tie an OVERHAND KNOT in the *working part* about where you want the loop to begin. Form the loop and thread the *working end* through the OVERHAND KNOT. Now tie a HALF KNOT with the *working end* around the *working part* close to the OVERHAND KNOT. Draw up both knots, and then draw the two

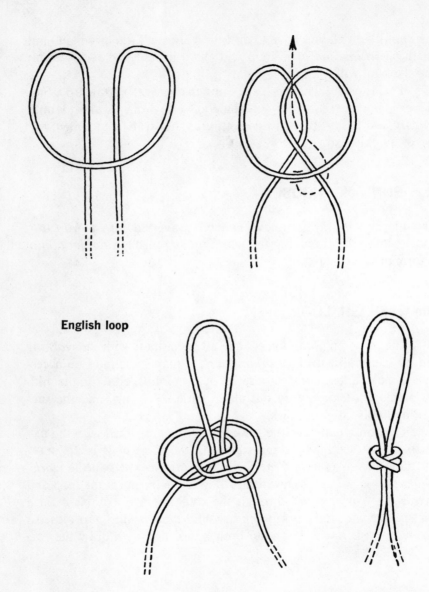

English loop

tightly together by pulling on the loop and the two legs of the *work-*
ing part.

That's the obvious way to tie it, but it means you may have to thread perhaps as much as half the whole length of cord, first through the initial OVERHAND KNOT, and then again through the *crossed loop* in making the following HALF KNOT.

There's a quicker way to tie the ENGLISH LOOP which avoids this difficulty. It sounds a bit complicated in the description, but the drawing, I think, makes it clear.

Make an *open loop* in the cord about where you want the final loop to be. Hold the two legs of the *working part* loosely in the left hand. With the right hand, pull the top of the loop back over the two legs of the *working part,* so that you have made two *crossed loops* opposite each other. Hold the crossing steady under your left thumb. Now pass the right-hand leg of the *working part* to the left and over the left-hand leg, so that the two loops are now crossing each other as well as the two legs of the *working part.* Now pull the bottom of the original loop down between the two legs of the *work-ing part* and then upward and through the space made by the two opposing loops when you crossed them. Draw the loop on through to the length required, then work the knot tight with the fingers.

This makes a very strong and reliable *loop knot,* but is rather bulky. Also the two legs of the *working part* lead out of the knot in line with the two sides of the loop.

The LINEMAN'S LOOP

If you should want the two legs of the *working part* of the loop to

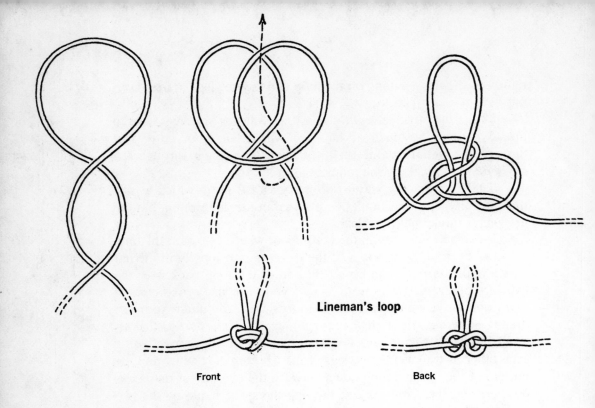

Lineman's loop

Front   Back

lead away from it in opposite directions and at right angles to it, the LINEMAN'S LOOP solves the problem.

Form a *crossed loop* and hold it in the left hand just as you did the *open loop* to start the ENGLISH LOOP. With the right hand give the loop a half twist, so that you have formed a figure eight with the cord above the left thumb. Bring the top of the loop back down over the crossing in the *working part* as for the ENGLISH LOOP, down between the legs of the *working part* below the crossing, and then upward through the space made by the lower half of the figure eight.

Draw the loop out to the desired length. The knot is drawn up by taking a leg of the *working part* in each hand and pulling to right and left in line with each other, working the knot with the fingers as necessary to shape it.

Once you have learned the trick of them, both these knots are very quickly tied. They are a bit slower to untie, as both have a tendency to jam under heavy strain. With both knots the easiest way to loosen them is to hold the knot in the left hand, and with the right hand work both legs of the loop simultaneously backward through the knot.

The FARMER'S LOOP

The FARMER'S LOOP is another which has a good lead at right angles to the loop. It is tied in a quick and most ingenious way.

Lead the *working end* of the cord over the left thumb from front to back, and with it take TWO ROUND TURNS around the thumb. You will now have three turns facing you. With the thumb and forefinger of the right hand, nip the middle turn of the three and "jump" it to the right over the right-hand turn.

Again nip the middle turn (the original right-hand turn) with the right forefinger and thumb, and this time jump it to the left over the left-hand turn. This now becomes the middle turn. Once more pinch the middle turn with the right forefinger and thumb, and jump it again to the right. Now you have a new turn in the middle. Draw it out to form the loop. Slide the knot off your thumb, draw out the loop to the size you want it while the knot is still loose, and then draw up the knot by pulling on both *working parts* in opposite directions. The knot may need some working into shape with your fingers while it is being drawn up.

The description may sound a little complicated, but once you have got the hang of it, this knot can be tied so quickly that to an onlooker it will seem like a magician's trick. Jump right, jump left, jump right again, and draw out, always with the middle turn.

If you are making the loop in rope or heavy line, obviously you won't be able to do it over your thumb. Just use your left forearm in place of your thumb. But leave the knot slack enough so it will slide off over your hand.

If you want to hang out some clothes to air on coat hangers, and don't want them all bunched together because the hooks on the hangers tend to slide along the sagging line, tie as many FARMER'S LOOPS as you have hangers four to six inches apart in your clothesline, and hook the hangers in the loops.

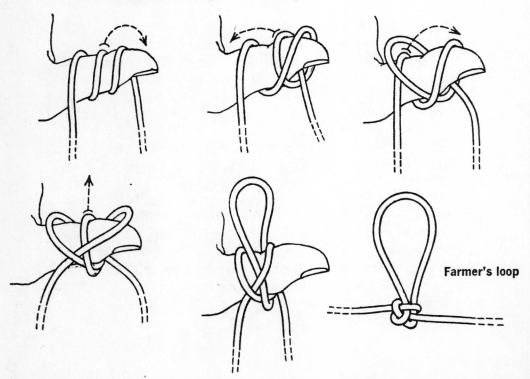

Farmer's loop

Chapter v ▪ The Hitches

A *hitch* is a knot which is made either around its own *working part,* or more commonly around another object, for the purpose of fastening the *working part* securely to the object. In most cases the object will be something like a post, a stake, the trunk or limb of a tree, a log or a piece of timber.

The SINGLE HITCH

The SINGLE HITCH is really nothing more than a *round turn* taken around an object, with the *working part* crossed over the *working end* and pinching the *working end* to the object. Loose, it is of course completely unstable. But if the strain on the *working part* is strong enough to keep the *working end* from slipping around the object, it will hold.

The SINGLE HITCH in its *slipped* form is known as the SLIP-PERY HITCH. Ashley describes it as the answer to the problem the sailor sets the landsman: "How would you lower yourself from the edge of a precipice, with a rope just long enough to reach the ground below, and then continue on your way carrying your rope with you?" Answer: Make a SLIPPERY HITCH by turning the *working end* of your rope back on itself and making a SINGLE HITCH over it around the trunk or branch of a tree on the edge of the precipice. When you have climbed down and reach the ground, you give the rope a flip, and the hitch falls free. Me, I think I'd rather just jump off the cliff, and get it all over quickly.

The BLACKWALL HITCH (see p. 93) is a SINGLE HITCH tied around the shank of a hook.

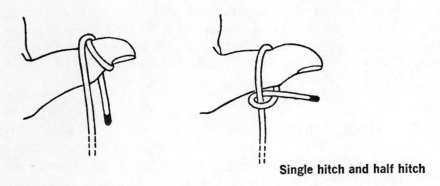

Single hitch and half hitch

The HALF HITCH

The HALF HITCH has already been described in Chapter II (see p. 37). Here it is only necessary to reiterate that it is tied in exactly the same way as the HALF KNOT, except that in the HALF KNOT the *working end* comes out of the knot in the opposite direction from the *working part,* and in line with it, whereas in the HALF HITCH the *working end* comes out of the knot more or less at right angles to the *working part.*

The SLIPPED HALF HITCH

Normally the HALF HITCH is so easy to untie that it doesn't require any treatment to make it easier. However, if the occasion should arise where you want to be able to free it instantly from whatever it is hitched to, make a *slipped knot* of it by turning the *working end* back on itself to make a *closed loop,* and use the loop to make the hitch. It will now spill by pulling on the *working end,* as with the other *slipped knots.*

TWO HALF HITCHES

To make TWO HALF HITCHES you simply add another HALF HITCH to the one already made. This knot is often used, made around its own *working part,* to complete the tying up of a parcel. When so used the two hitches can be made secure by tying a final OVERHAND KNOT close up to them. They are not so often used to secure the *working part* to an object like a stake or a post. The following knot is much more suitable for that purpose.

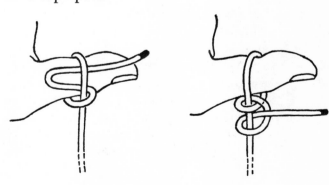

Slipped half hitch and two half hitches

With the *working end* take a *round turn* around the stake or post. Then add the TWO HALF HITCHES around the *working part*.

This is a very simple and secure *hitch,* quickly tied and untied. It may, if desirable, be made more secure by adding an OVERHAND KNOT in the *working end* as above.

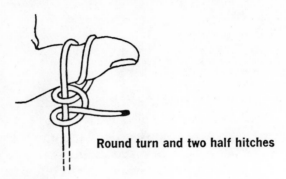

Round turn and two half hitches

The CLOVE HITCH

The easiest way to describe how to tie this *hitch* is to imagine yourself needing to fasten your cord to a horizontal bar, like the rail of a fence, for example.

Hold the *working part* in your left hand, and take a *single turn* over and around the bar with the *working end,* but so that the *working end* comes back to the left of the *working part.* Now take the *working end* over and around the bar again to the right of the first turn and pass it *under* the second turn. Now you have the *working end* coming out of the *hitch* in line with the *working part* and leading in the opposite direction. Both the *working end* and the *working part* lie between the turns.

Now if you want to tie your CLOVE HITCH around something that has one end you can get at, there's still an easier way to do it. Suppose you want to tie it around the top of a fence post. Take the *working part* in your left hand. Take the *working end* in your right hand, holding it with the palm downward. Now turn your right hand over, palm upward. You have made a *crossed loop*. Drop the *crossed loop* over the top of the post. Then repeat the process by making another *crossed loop* in the same way, and drop it over the post on top of the first loop. Draw up by pulling equally on the *working part* and the *working end*.

This is known as *"throwing"* the *hitch*. You can have fun practicing it using your left thumb as the top of the post, as shown in the drawing.

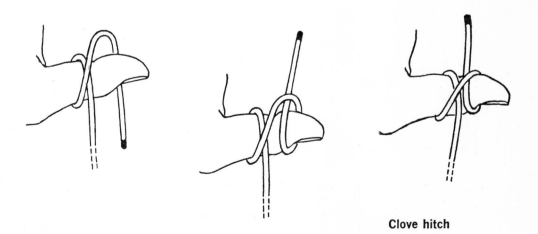

Clove hitch

The CLOVE HITCH is one of the most useful of the *hitches*. One of its virtues is that it will take a strain equally well on either the *working end* or the *working part* or on both simultaneously. Another is that, assuming it to have been drawn up tightly, it does not tend to slip along the length of whatever it has been tied around. Whether tied around something vertical, something horizontal, or something inclined, it will not slip along it, provided the strain on the *hitch* is at, or nearly at, right angles to the something around which it has been tied.

The CLOVE HITCH will always remain secure so long as there is a strain upon it. But it can work loose when the strain is taken off it. If this is likely to happen use the CLOVE HITCH SECURED.

The CLOVE HITCH SECURED

Simply take a HALF HITCH with the *working end* around the *working part*.

The CLOVE HITCH is easy to loosen and untie by pushing either the *working end* or the *working part* back under its own turn.

But if you want to be able to free it in a hurry, you can make the SLIPPED CLOVE HITCH.

The SLIPPED CLOVE HITCH

When you come to the stage of passing the *working end* under and through the second turn, double the *working end* back on itself to form a *closed loop,* and pass the *closed loop* under and through the

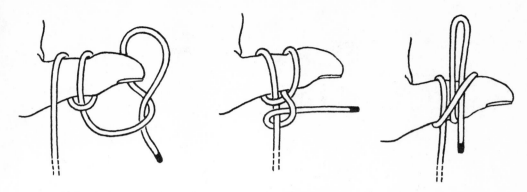

| "Throwing" the clove hitch | Clove hitch secured | Slipped clove hitch |

turn. Now the *working end* will come out alongside the *working part* and leading in the same direction. Now you can free the hitch by pulling on the *working end*. Of course in this case only the *working part* can take any strain.

The RING HITCH

This, as its name implies, is a useful knot if you want to attach your cord to a ring of any size, or to something similar, like the loop in another piece of cord.

Take the *working end* back along the *working part* to form a *closed loop* at the point you want to attach the ring. Pass the loop through the ring, and open it out enough so that the ring can pass through the loop. Holding on to the ring, pull on the doubled cord until the *hitch* comes up snug on the ring.

Like the CLOVE HITCH, the RING HITCH is composed of two *crossed loops*. But in the CLOVE HITCH, each of the loops is made in

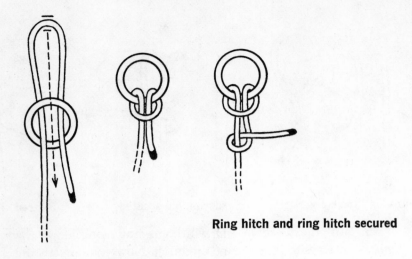

Ring hitch and ring hitch secured

the same way. In the RING HITCH, the second loop is made in re-verse, so that the *working end* and the *working part* come out lead-ing in the same direction, whereas in the CLOVE HITCH the *working end* and *working part* come out of the hitch leading in opposite di-rections.

When used over a stake or post or similar object, the RING HITCH is often called a COW HITCH.

The RING HITCH SECURED

If you want the strain to come on only one part of the cord, you can secure it in the same way as the CLOVE HITCH by taking a HALF HITCH with the part on which there will be no strain around the part which will be under strain.

The MIDSHIPMAN'S HITCH

There are very few knots indeed which can be tied under tension—
that is, when there is already a strain on the *working part* which
must be maintained while the knot is being completed. This is one
of them.

Let's assume you want to rig a clothesline between two posts in
the garden, and you want the line to be as taut as possible so that it
won't sag under the weight of the wet washing. Secure one end of
your line to one post with any of the *loop knots* or *hitches*. Take
your line to the other post and make a *single turn* around it. Now
haul on the line until you have got it as taut as you can. Maintain
the strain on the line with your left hand, but leaving enough of the
working end free to make the *hitch*. With the right hand, take a
HALF HITCH with the *working end* around the *working part*. Now
pass the *working end* once more around the *working part,* to the left
of the *hitch,* and bring it up through the loop that has been formed
around the post. Holding the *working end* taut with the right hand,
with the left slide the two turns to the left along the working part
until the strain comes equally on both sides of the loop, and the line
is as taut as you can make it. Keeping the HALF HITCH with its
added turn in place with the left hand, take another HALF HITCH
with the *working end* around the *working part* to the left—or away
from the post—and pull up tight.

The MIDSHIPMAN'S HITCH is not nearly so complicated as you
might imagine from the verbal description. But if you will study the
diagram I think you will find it fairly simple.

When you examine the completed knot, you will see that the
effect of the two turns inside the HALF HITCH is to kink the *working*

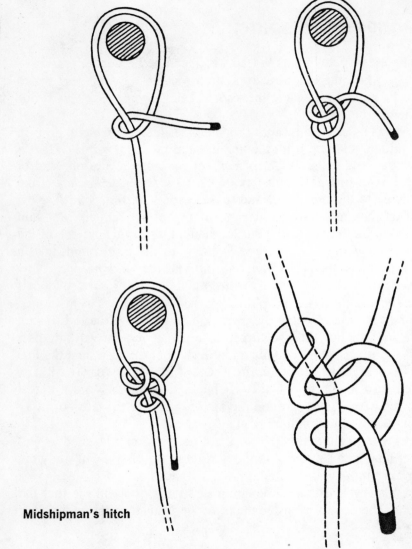

Midshipman's hitch

part in such a way that the turns will not slip along it and so cause
the cord to slacken. To make it clear, I have shown the knot magni-
fied in the drawing, the dotted lines indicating the way the knot puts
the kink in the *working part.*

As long as the strain on it is maintained, the MIDSHIPMAN'S
HITCH will keep the line under its original tension practically forever. But of course if the line should stretch, and so slacken the tension, the *hitch* may slip. But even if it does, you can always tauten
the line up again by untying the last HALF HITCH, sliding the turns
back along the working part until the tension is as you want it, and
securing again with the HALF HITCH.

The MIDSHIPMAN'S HITCH can be, quite literally, a life-saver.
If you fall overboard, and someone throws you a line, grab it with
your left hand, and pass the end of the line around your waist with
your right hand. Make the first two HALF HITCHES with your right
hand above your left hand, i.e. toward the boat. Haul the hitches
tight, away from you, with your right hand. Now, let go with your
left hand, and with it slide the hitches toward you until the loop is
snug—but not too snug—around your waist. Holding the hitches
firmly with your left hand, with your right hand pass the third
HALF HITCH around the *working part* to make the knot secure.
Haul up on the *working end,* marry it to the *working part* leading
toward the boat and, as an added precaution, hold the married
parts tightly with both hands. Now you're ready to be hauled
safely aboard.

The same method can be used in a mountaineering accident to
rescue a climber who has fallen—assuming of course he is not so
badly injured as to be incapable of making the hitch.

Chapter vi ∎ The Bends

A *bend* is a knot which securely attaches the end of one piece of cord or rope to the end of another, separate, piece of cord or rope. The most frequent use for a *bend* is to make one longer piece of cord or rope out of two or more shorter pieces of the same size. Or a *bend* may be used to join a piece of cord or rope to another of larger or smaller size.

The OVERHAND BEND

There is a right way and a wrong way to tie the OVERHAND BEND. The wrong way is to put the two *working ends* together, leading in the same direction, and then tie an OVERHAND KNOT in them. If you do this, and then open out the *working parts* to lead in opposite directions, and put a strain on the joined cords, one of two things is bound to happen. Either the knot will spill, or it will jam.

The right way is to tie an OVERHAND KNOT loosely in one *working end*. Then pass the other *working end* through, exactly paralleling the first *working end* but in the opposite direction, thus making a second OVERHAND KNOT within the first. Now the two

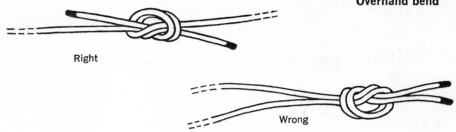

Right

Wrong

working parts lead out of the knot correctly in line with each other and in opposite directions, as do the two *working ends.* The strain is now taken by the joined cords, and is not borne entirely by the knot, as in the wrong version.

The only case in which the wrong OVERHAND BEND is allowable is when you want to secure two pieces of cord together to double the strength of the cord, if it is too light to take the strain that may be put upon it. This is permissible because—and only because—in that case any strain will come on the doubled cord, and not on the knot itself.

The ENGLISH BEND

This is a good *bend,* both because it is strong and secure, and because the lead of the two *working parts* is right, coming out of the knot in opposite directions, so that the strain on either side of the knot is equalized.

With the *working end* of one piece of cord, tie a HALF KNOT around the *working part* of the other piece. With the *working end* of

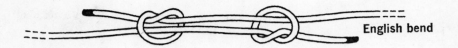

English bend

the other piece, tie a HALF KNOT around the *working part* of the first piece of cord. Draw both HALF KNOTS up tight, then complete drawing up the whole knot by pulling on both *working parts* in opposite directions, thus snugging the two HALF KNOTS together.

It is a fairly easy knot to untie, too. If you pull on the two *working ends,* the HALF KNOTS will slide apart, and are then readily loosened.

The ENGLISH BEND SECURED

The ENGLISH BEND is a pretty reliable knot as it stands, but if you want to make assurance doubly sure, leave the *working ends* long enough so that with each you can take a HALF HITCH around its opposing *working part.*

English bend secured

The BOWLINE BEND

If it's security you want above all else, then quite the safest arrangement is the BOWLINE BEND.

Tie a BOWLINE in the *working end* of one piece of your cord. Pass the *working end* of the other piece through the loop of the

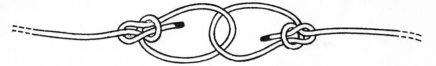

BOWLINE, and in it tie another BOWLINE. You will now have your two pieces of cord joined by the two loops, as it might be by the links in a chain. This *bend* is particularly useful in heavier stuff, stout rope which is to take a strong strain, for example. It is also probably the best *bend* to use when joining two ropes of unequal size.

The SHEET BEND

This is a very simple and practical *bend,* quite reliable if it has been drawn up really tight, but with a tendency to slip if it hasn't.

If you will look at the diagram you will see that the knot itself is exactly the same construction as the BOWLINE, except that it is made with the *working ends* of two pieces of cord instead of only one, and it is tied in the same way, with one small difference.

Instead of taking the *working part* of the cord in your left hand, as you would to start the BOWLINE, you take the *working end* of one piece of cord in the left hand, palm downward, and the *working end* of the other piece in the right hand, palm downward, with the *working parts* leading in opposite directions.

Now lay the *working end* of the piece in your right hand over the piece in the left hand, right forefinger extended, push down a little, bring the left hand slightly forward, and turn both hands palm

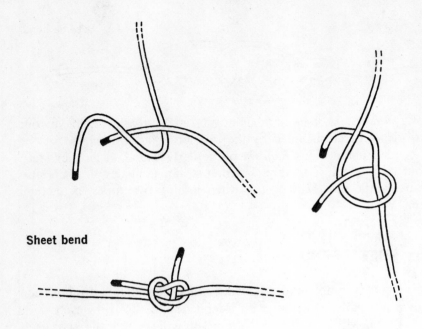

Sheet bend

upward. Now you've made a small *crossed loop* in the first piece of cord, with the *working end* of the second piece threaded through the *crossed loop* from below upward.

Then, just as for the BOWLINE, pass the *working end* to the left around behind the *working part* of the first piece, and down through the *crossed loop* alongside and parallel with its own *working part*.

And, as with the BOWLINE, you have made a HALF HITCH with the *working end* of the first piece around a *closed loop* in the second piece, with the *working part* of the first piece threaded through the *closed loop*.

The SHEET BEND is just as easy to untie as the BOWLINE, and

done the same way, by pushing the *working part* in which the HALF
HITCH has been made, backward through the *closed loop*.

The BOWLINE and the SHEET BEND are both made by passing the *working end* from right to left around behind the *working part* and down through the *crossed loop*. When made this way they are called a "right-hand" BOWLINE and a "right-hand" SHEET BEND respectively. If the *working ends* are passed around behind the *working parts* in the opposite direction, that is from left to right, and then down through the *crossed loop,* they are known as a "left-hand" BOWLINE and a "left-hand" SHEET BEND. Although the two versions look so alike, and seem to be constructed in the same way, for some reason and in both cases the "left-hand" version is very much inferior to the "right-hand." Though the reason isn't apparent, security tests done by subjecting the knot to repeated even jerks on the *working parts* show the "left-hand" versions of both knots tend to slip nearly twice as often as the "right-hand" versions. So avoid tying a "left-hand" BOWLINE and a "left-hand" SHEET BEND as you would avoid tying a GRANNY KNOT.

The PARCEL BEND

This is a very simple and practical *bend* for knotting together two pieces of thin string or twine.

Hold the *working end* of one piece in the left hand. With the right hand make a CROSSING KNOT with the second piece around the first, by taking its *working end* over and then back under the first piece, upward over its own *working part,* across it, and under the first piece again. Pinching the CROSSING KNOT firmly between the thumb and forefinger of the left hand, with the right hand pass a

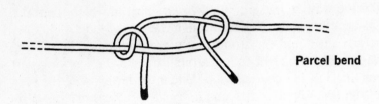

Parcel bend

HALF HITCH around the *working part* of the second piece with the *working end* of the first piece. Draw the HALF HITCH up tight against the CROSSING KNOT.

The advantage of this *bend* is that it can be tied and drawn up while one of the pieces is under tension. The next time you find you have almost finished tying up a parcel, but haven't allowed yourself quite enough string to finish the job, just cut off another piece, start a PARCEL BEND, but before you pass the HALF HITCH, draw up tautly on the string already around the parcel, and with it snug the HALF HITCH up against the CROSSING KNOT you have made with your additional piece. Very neat, very effective.

The RUBBER BAND BEND

Have you ever needed a rubber band to go around a bundle of paper or letters or something similar, and not been able to find a long enough one in the house?

Take your small rubber bands and link them together by making a *closed loop* of one and an *open loop* of another, pass the *closed loop* through the *open loop,* bring the *closed loop* back, open it, and pass the other end of its band through and draw up. This is exactly the same procedure as for the RING HITCH, but when you

stretch the two bands they will tend to fall into the same shape as a
SQUARE KNOT. Repeat the process until you have made a chain of rubber bands long enough to take your bundle. Then join the two ends of the chain with a SHEET BEND.

It sounds a bit silly, I suppose, to dignify anything so absurdly simple by calling it a knot. But it can come in very handy if it's needed.

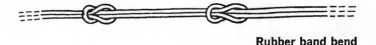

Rubber band bend

Chapter vii ▪ Some Special Purpose Knots

Most of the knots described in the preceding pages might be called general utility knots—that is, they can be used in a variety of ways for a variety of purposes. There are also some knots which are designed to be used for one particular purpose only—a purpose for which no other knot will serve as satisfactorily.

Here are a few of them.

The SHEEPSHANK

The purpose of the SHEEPSHANK is to shorten a length of rope or cord which is too long for the job in hand, but which you do not want to cut to the right length, thereby perhaps wasting some of it.

Take your length of rope, and estimate roughly how long you want it to be. Middle it—that is, bring the two ends together to form a long loop. Take the two legs of the loop in the left hand at a distance from the ends equal to about half the length you want the rope to be. With the right hand lead one leg of the loop back alongside the loop to form two *closed loops* with the ends leading in opposite directions. With the part of the cord lying next to it, throw a

Sheepshank

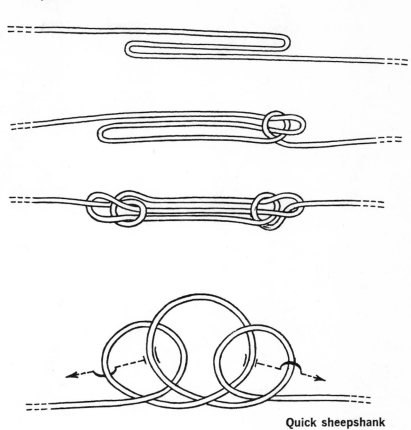

Quick sheepshank

HALF HITCH around the right-hand loop and quite close to the end of the loop. Pass the *working end* of the rope through the loop and draw the HALF HITCH up tight. Reverse the knot, and do the same to the other loop with the other end of the rope, passing a HALF HITCH around the loop, threading the end through it, and drawing up tight.

If the rope is now either a little too long or a little too short for your purpose, you can shorten it or lengthen it by loosening the HALF HITCHES and making the two loops longer or shorter as desired.

There is a quick, trick way of making the SHEEPSHANK. Make a coil of three overlapping *crossed loops,* a small one to the left, a larger one in the middle, and another smaller one to the right. With the forefingers and thumbs of both hands, draw the right side of the larger loop through the small loop to its right, and the left side of the larger loop through the small loop to its left. Keep on drawing up equally right and left until all of the slack of the larger loop has been taken up, then pass the two ends through the loops as above to secure the HALF HITCHES to the loops.

The SHEEPSHANK is quite often shown without the additional security of passing the ends through the loops. But without that added precaution the SHEEPSHANK is highly unstable, particularly if it is subjected to sudden repeated slackening and tautening, as it might be if it were used, say, to shorten a tow-rope on an automobile or tractor. It is safest always to tie the SHEEPSHANK as described above, which makes a completely secure knot of it.

The two following knots are particularly adapted for use with hooks, either when hanging something from a hook, or using a hook at the end of a rope over a pulley, as it might be for hoisting bales of hay or sacks of grain or feed up into the hayloft of a barn.

The BLACKWALL HITCH

This is simply a SINGLE HITCH taken around the shank of the hook, as shown in the drawing.

Despite its unsafe appearance, it is quite secure *as long as* there is a strain on the working part of the rope. It will spill or slip at once if the strain is taken off. Because it can be so easily shaken free of the hook when the strain on the rope is slackened, it is much used in loading and unloading cargo from ships or lighters.

It can be secured quite simply by adding two HALF HITCHES around the *working part* below the hook.

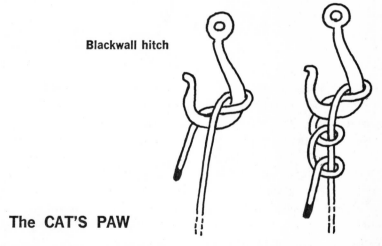

Blackwall hitch

The CAT'S PAW

This is a way of fastening a rope or cord to a hook, either temporarily or permanently, to avoid any risk that the hook might chafe through the rope, as would be possible if it were put over the hook singly.

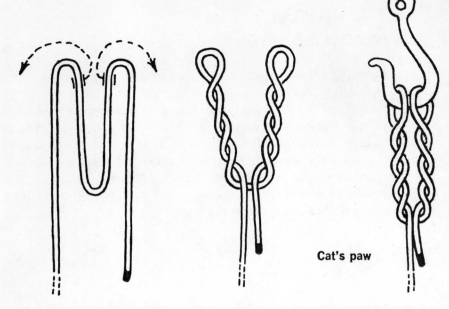

Cat's paw

Turn back a couple of feet or more of the rope on itself to form a *closed loop*. Turn the loop back on itself once more to form two *closed loops*. Twist each loop two or three times, one loop clockwise, the other counterclockwise. Slip both loops over the hook.

The CAT'S PAW is most frequently made when using a *sling* to hoist a bale or sack or barrel or other heavy object. A *sling* is a piece of rope whose ends have been either knotted or spliced together to make one continuous loop. When the CAT'S PAW is used with a *sling* the strain will, of course, be distributed equally between the two parts of the rope coming out of the knot. If the strain is only going to come on the *working part* of the rope, then it is wise to secure the CAT'S PAW by taking a HALF HITCH with the *working end*

around the *working part* just below the knot. Or you can make a
HALF KNOT with the *working end* around both the *working part* and
the bottom loop of the CAT'S PAW.

   If you occasionally have to carry something heavy and awkwardly shaped, like a box, or a case of liquor or beer, or the like, make yourself a *sling*. Get a piece of braided clothes line or thin rope. Cut off seven or eight feet. Join the two ends with an ENGLISH BEND, leaving the ends nine or ten inches long outside the bend. Draw up the bend, then make as many HALF HITCHES around the *working parts* on either side as the length of the ends will allow. Marry the *working ends* to the *working parts,* and put on *seizings* to make all secure. Now you can use the *sling* to make a RING HITCH around the box or case, pulling the bend through the loop. The bend will then make a comfortable carrying handle.

The TIMBER HITCH

The TIMBER HITCH is also known as the LUMBERMAN'S KNOT or the COUNTRYMAN'S KNOT.

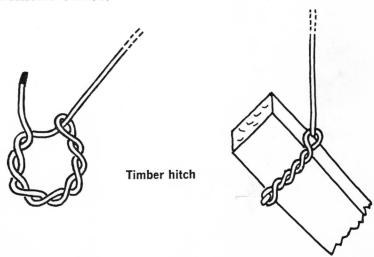

Timber hitch

It is a very good *hitch* if you have to hoist, or carry, or drag a big log, a branch of a tree, a heavy plank of beam, or some similar awkward object.

Let's say it is a heavy plank. Take a HALF HITCH loosely around it. Then take half-a-dozen or more turns with the *working end* back around itself in the direction in which the *working part* is leading around the plank.

Pull on the *working part* until the *hitch* is drawn up very snug. The twist in the rope will keep the *hitch* from sliding along the plank in either direction, *as long as* there is a strain on the *working part*. With a TIMBER HITCH you can safely hoist any heavy object, the mast or spar of a boat, say, or a big beam or heavy post, whether it is round or square or some other shape in cross-section, and even if the *hitch* has to be made fairly close to one of its ends.

It cannot jam, and is very easily freed by pushing the *working part* back through the loop. You may not find you have to use this *hitch* very often around the house, but when you need it, no other knot will serve.

The SHORT END BEND

The end result of this knot is identical with the SHEET BEND (see p. 85). But because it serves one special purpose, and because of the ingenious way in which it is tied, I think it deserves inclusion in this chapter.

You want to fasten, *bend,* two pieces of cord together. But for some reason one end is too short to be tied with any of the conventional *bends*. (A good example is a broken shoelace, where a short bit protrudes from an eyelet, and you don't want to take the time to undo the whole lace, knot it, and then lace the shoe up again.)

Make a SLIPKNOT in the end of the longer piece, tighten it, and draw it up so the loop is just big enough to slip over the short end. Thread the short end through the loop of the SLIPKNOT and push the loop down as far as the short end will allow. Tighten the SLIP-KNOT on the short end. Now pull gently and equally in opposite directions on the *working end* and the *working part* of the longer piece. As you do, the SLIPKNOT will appear to "swallow" the short end, and when the whole knot is securely tightened, it will look exactly like the SHEET BEND.

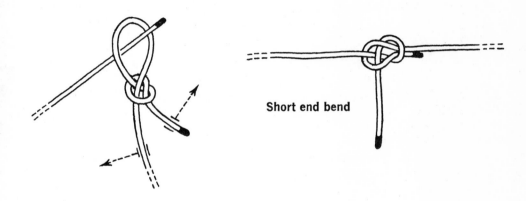

Short end bend

Chapter viii ▪ *Practical Applications*

Tying Up Parcels

Kipling wrote:

> "There are nine and sixty ways
> Of composing tribal lays
> And every single one of them is right."

There are nine-and-ninety ways of tying up parcels. And ninety-eight of them are wrong.

Before you start doing up your parcel, you should measure the paper and string you will need.

Spread the paper out on a table or bench or kitchen counter. Put your parcel on it. Fold the near side of the paper over the top, positioning the parcel so that the near edge of the paper just reaches the far side of the parcel. Fold the far edge of the paper back over the parcel toward you. Where it reaches the near side of the parcel crease it to mark where you will cut it. Open the paper out again, and position the parcel so that the left side of the parcel is at a distance from the edge of the paper just a little less than the depth of the parcel. With a crease or a snip of the scissors mark off an equal distance on the paper from the right end of the parcel. Now cut the right side of the paper, as straight as you can by eye, from the near side to the crease you have made on the far side. Cut along that crease from right to left to complete the cutting out.

To measure the amount of string or twine you will need, first decide how many turns you will want to put on to make the parcel secure. If it is fairly small and square or nearly square, two turns will probably be enough—that is, one turn around the parcel in one direction, and another at right angles to the first. If the parcel is rectangular, and its length is rather more than its breadth, you will need more turns, one around its longer dimension, two or perhaps three around its shorter dimension. If the parcel is very long and narrow, a rolled-up rug for example, you may need a number of turns, perhaps as many as seven or eight.

Let us suppose you decide to put on three turns—that is, one lengthways and two around its breadth. Take the *working end* of the string between the left forefinger and thumb, and hold it at the *bottom* of the left side of the parcel. With the right forefinger and thumb measure the string to the *top* of the right side of the parcel. Move your left forefinger and thumb to take the place of the right forefinger and thumb, and repeat the measurement. Now you have measured off enough string to take your turn around the length of the parcel. Do the same for the crossing turns, measuring from the lower front edge of the parcel over the top to the upper back edge. Do this four times, and you will have enough string to make the two crossing turns. Cut the string about a foot beyond this point, to allow for the expenditure on the knots.

(You can do all this in about a quarter of the time it has taken you to read my explanation. And you will not leave yourself with three or four feet of wasted string, or worse still, find you have cut your string a foot too short.)

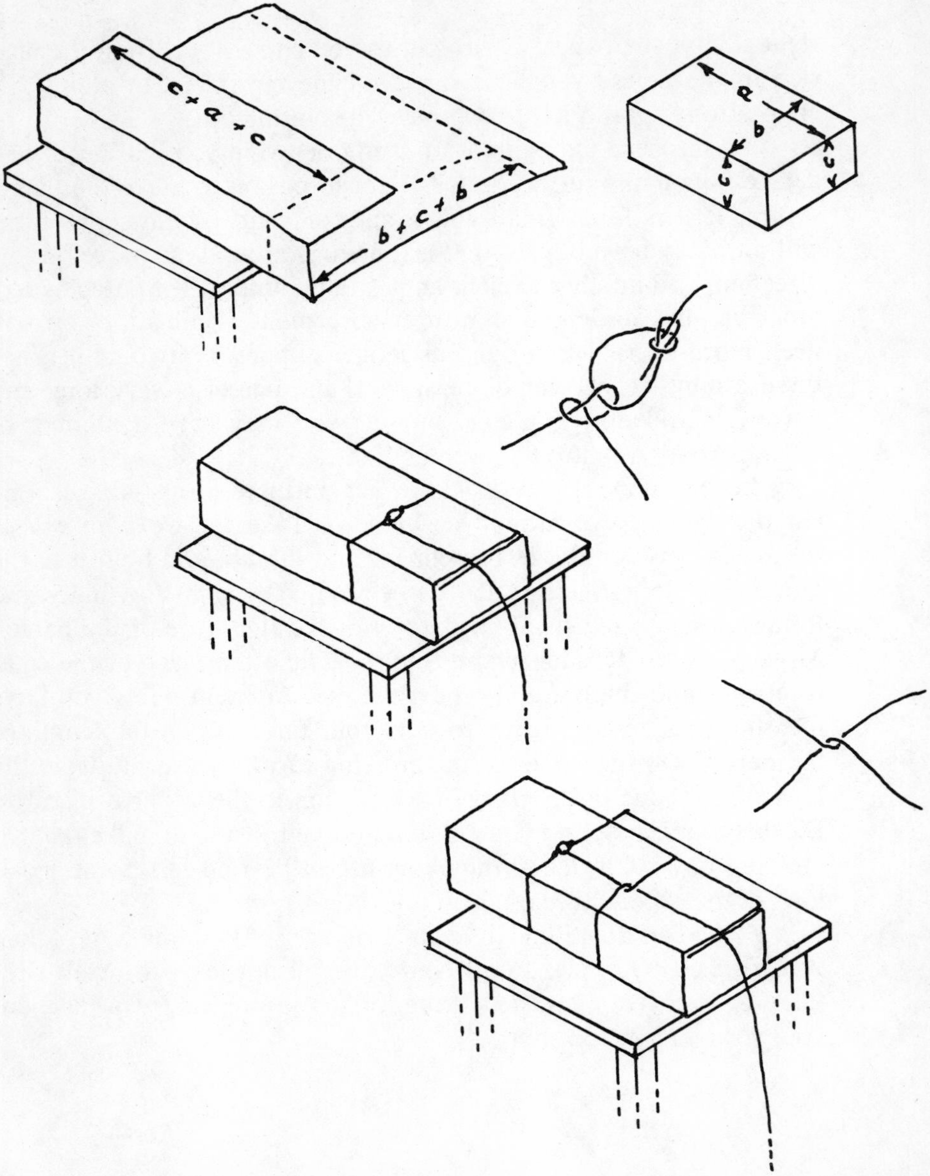

$c + a + c$

$b + c + b$

a

b

c

c

Now tie a LOOP KNOT about an inch long in the *working end*
of the string. You can use any of the suitable LOOP KNOTS, but
you'll do best always to use a BOWLINE, especially if your parcel is
likely to get rough handling, since it is the most secure.

Position the parcel on the paper. Fold the front edge of the paper over the parcel from front to back, then do likewise with the far
edge, folding it from back to front. Holding the paper in place with
the left hand, hold the LOOP KNOT with the left thumb and forefinger, while with your right hand you take the first turn around the
parcel with the *working part* of the string. Pass the *working part*
through the loop to form a RUNNING NOOSE (see p. 65) and draw
up tight around the parcel. Secure the *working part* to the loop with
a HALF HITCH. The turn should be positioned about a third of the
way—or a little less—along the length of the parcel from the right
end. And be sure the string goes round the parcel straight, at right
angles to the length of the parcel. Otherwise the turn will not be
tight.

Turn the parcel right round end for end, so that the first turn is
to the left, lead the *working part* of the string to the right, make an
elbow in it with the left hand, and with the right take another turn
around the parcel and make a HAMMOCK HITCH (see p. 40)
through the elbow, taking the *working part* of the string *over* the
elbow and out to the right *under* it. Draw up loosely.

Now, using both hands, you can fold the paper over the right
end of the parcel as shown in the drawing. First fold downward over
the top edge, then fold inward over it the two triangles of paper
which have been made at front and back, crease them well down,
and fold the remainder upward from the bottom edge. Take the
string around the end of the parcel, then turn the parcel over, so
that the bottom is now on top. Lead the string back to the left and

make CROSSING KNOTS (see p. 38) with the *working part* around the crossing turns. Turn the parcel end for end again and fold the paper at the remaining end as you did with the first. Turn the parcel over, bring the string around the end, and back to the LOOP KNOT. Thread the *free end* through the loop, take it over the lengthwise part, under the *working part* leading to the right, then back alongside itself, and draw all up taut, if necessary tightening up both the lengthwise and the crossing turns in order of tying. Now take two HALF HITCHES around the working part and secure the two HALF HITCHES with an OVERHAND KNOT close up to the last hitch. Two HALF HITCHES are all that is necessary. Many people seem to think that the more HALF HITCHES they put on the securer the parcel will be. It won't, and they are just wasting their time and string and the time and temper of whoever has to untie the parcel at the other end.

There are two useful variations on the above method. If the parcel is not likely to get much rough handling, and you want to be able to undo it easily, use a SLIPPED BOWLINE (see p. 64) for your LOOP KNOT. (Though I have found a SLIPPED BOWLINE a fairly secure knot under most circumstances, I don't know that I would trust it to stand up to the kind of treatment parcels get in post offices or baggage check rooms.) Finish the tying with two SLIPPED HALF HITCHES. Now by slipping both knots simultaneously both ends of the string will come free at the same time.

And if the parcel is rather heavy and you want to be able to carry it without the string cutting into your hands, you can put on a carrying handle this way: Cut your string four or five feet longer than you need for actually tying the parcel. When you have put on the two final HALF HITCHES, expend the remaining length of string by weaving it back and forth around the crossing turns—taking the end under the crossing part, over the lengthwise part and back un-

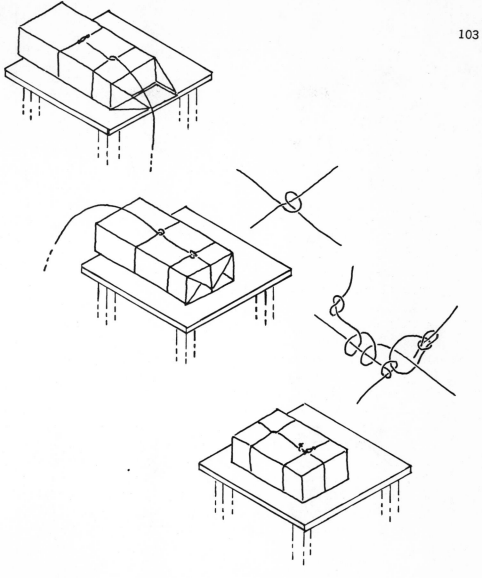

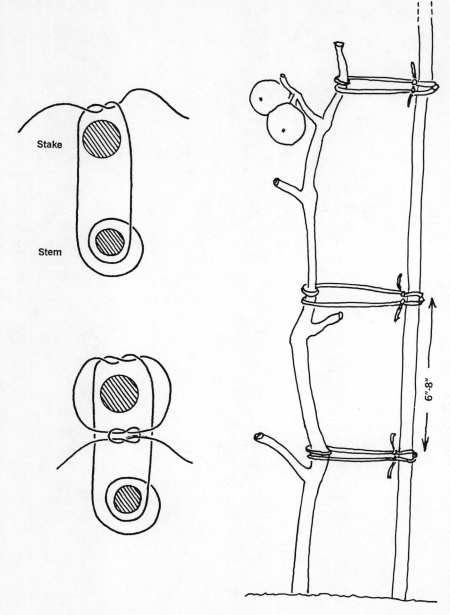

Stake

Stem

6"-8"

der the crossing part on the other side, leading it back and doing the same at the first crossing, and repeating until you have only a foot or so of string left. With it take as many turns as you can around the back-and-forth weaving, and finish at the crossing with two more HALF HITCHES and an OVERHAND KNOT to secure them. This will make quite a comfortable handle.

Here is a hint if you want to tie up a cardboard carton which has already been opened. Most such cartons open down the middle of the top. If you make your initial lengthwise turn around the top and the bottom, the string is liable to slip between the two edges of the top opening and cut down into the ends of the carton. Take your LOOP KNOT at the beginning to the middle of one *side* of the carton (if you can turn the carton on its side to do this, it is easier) and proceed from there, so that the lengthwise turn is taken around the girth of the carton, as it were, instead of over the top and under the bottom.

Tying Up Plants in the Garden

The main thing to remember when tying up almost anything that grows in the garden, whether to a stake, a trellis, a fence, or any other kind of support, is that the stem of the plant or vine or bush or tree *must* have freedom to expand as it grows. Otherwise whatever it is tied with will cut into the stem or bark, scarring it, and preventing the sap from rising properly to the top leaves and branches.

Probably the best material to use for tying up any tender-stemmed plants is the gardener's old stand-by, raffia. It is soft and supple enough to be kind to the plant, but strong and durable enough to last a full growing season. Cord or string or twine is acceptable, if it

Stake

Trunk

is soft enough and thick enough not to cut into the stem. Any kind of wire is to be abhorred and avoided like the plague, even the plastic-covered wire or strips of paper with wire inside which are so often sold in garden shops for the purpose. Plants are even tenderer-skinned than you are, and how would you like to have a piece of wire twisted tightly round your arm, cutting off the circulation to your hand?

Whatever material you use, it is better to have a pair of scissors to cut it with than a knife, simply because with scissors you can cut your raffia or twine one-handed; with a knife you have to use both hands, one to hold the raffia, the other to hold the knife. A pair of short blunt-nosed scissors is best, then you can drop them in a pocket without fear either of stabbing yourself or punching a hole in your jacket.

As good an example as any to illustrate the basic method of tying up plants is a row of young tomato plants.

First drive your canes or stakes well into the ground several inches away from the stem of each plant, far enough away so the stake will not damage the roots.

Cut off a piece of raffia a foot or so long. With it take a loose *round turn* around the stem of the plant, and bring the two ends back around the stake, one on each side of it. Take them around the stake until they meet, and tie a HALF KNOT. Bring them around once more to meet again opposite the HALF KNOT, and finish with a SQUARE KNOT. The combination of the HALF KNOT and the SQUARE KNOT will enable you to tie the raffia tightly enough around the stake so it will not slip downward, without bringing any pressure to bear on the stem of the plant. And the loose *round turn* will let the stem expand freely while the plant is making its growth. If possible, it is best to put the *round turn* on just above a leaf or branch, to prevent it too from slipping downward.

This method of tying is applicable to all the smaller plants, to grapevines, roses, climbers like clematis or wisteria, and to every kind of support, stake, trellis, fence, or wires on a wall.

But *don't* make the tie too short. The stem needs room to move as it grows, especially when it is breezy, as well as to expand inside the tie itself. And use plenty of ties, one every few inches if necessary, so that the stem gets good support from the stakes.

The taller plants, sapling trees, young fruit trees, or large standard roses, obviously will require something stronger than a single strand of raffia. You can of course lay up ten or a dozen strands of raffia and twist them tightly together to make a stronger tie. But probably the best material is a length of old rope of appropriate size —within reason, the thicker the better, as being less likely to chafe the bark—which has become well worn and smooth with use. (New rope, whether hemp or sisal, has a surface like sandpaper.)

You will need a good stout stake, long enough so that when well driven into the ground the top of it will come just above where the tree starts to branch. Measure off your piece of rope so that you can take a *round turn* around the trunk of the tree, and come back to the stake with four or five inches to spare at each end.

Make your *round turn,* bring the two ends back on either side of the stake, and put on a *seizing* (see p. 123) with strong twine around the two ends of rope *between* the stake and trunk. Then similarly *seize* the two ends on the opposite side of the stake as close to it as possible. If the loop around the stake shows any tendency to slip downward, secure it in the right position by driving a short nail or wire staple through the rope into the stake. Then trim off the ends of the second *seizing* to make all tidy.

You can, if you like, substitute a RING HITCH for the *round turn*. It will not look quite as neat, but it does have the advantage

that you can put it on the trunk tightly enough initially so that the 109
hitch will not slide down the trunk, as the loose *round turn* will tend
to do, yet at the same time it will allow the trunk to expand without
constriction as it forces open the hitch. But *don't* use a CLOVE
HITCH for this purpose—as the trunk grows it will merely tighten
the hitch.

Knots in the Kitchen

It is always useful, I think, to have a ball of fairly fine twine or
string somewhere handy in the kitchen. But it can become a nui-
sance if it is just thrown loose into the back of a drawer to make a
tangle of itself.

Get a can, with a lid, just big enough to hold the ball of twine.
(One of those that cocktail nuts are sold in serves well.) Bore, or
punch, a hole in the center of the lid, and another in the center of
the bottom of the can. Find the end of twine that comes out of the
hole in the ball—*don't* use the end that has been wound round the
ball to hold it together. Cut off a couple of feet, middle it to form a
closed loop, and near the ends tie a *stopper knot* (OVERHAND KNOT
DOUBLED is the best). Thread the loop through the hole in the bottom of the can. Put the ball of twine in the can, and thread the end
of the twine through the hole in the lid. Replace the lid and secure it
to the can with a couple of turns of cellophane adhesive tape
(Scotch tape or suchlike). If you want to be really fancy, get a
small piece of the adhesive-backed plastic that is now sold everywhere and in such pleasant colors and designs for covering table
tops, kitchen counters, etc., and wrap it around the outside of the
can. But don't put it over the Scotch tape—you will need to be able

to remove that when your ball of string is used up and you want to replace it with a new one.

Now you can hang your can on a hook somewhere out of the way, behind a cupboard door, for example, and your string will always be handy when you need it.

One of the most frequent uses for string in the kitchen is—or should be—for tying up joints of meat or trussing fowls for roasting, either in the oven or on the spit. Every butcher, it seems to me, has his own pet way of tying a roast or trussing a chicken so that he can sell it "oven ready." Some even do it with a needle, so they can make the bird look as plump and attractive as possible to the customer. But pity the poor carver when the bird comes to the table. The string has become invisible in the roasting, and every time he makes a cut to take off a leg or a wing, he cuts another bit of string, and ends up with the platter littered untidily with the bits. And like as not, one of the guests will find himself chewing some along with his second joint.

The butchers do a little better with something like a rolled roast of beef, say. But even these are often so badly and sloppily tied that the roast will unroll itself in the cooking. In any case, any rolled roast, whether it be beef, boned shoulder of lamb, or a rolled roast of veal, is all the better for having its butcher's ties cut off, the roll opened out, and the inside well anointed with oil or butter, and spread with mixed herbs or rubbed with a clove of garlic, and then tied up again—properly.

Let's take a roast of beef as an example of how to do it—properly. When you have cut off the butcher's ties, spread the roast out and marinate it to your taste, roll it up again, and, if necessary, put a skewer through it to hold it while you put on the ties. Pass the string around the middle from front to back, and make a HALF

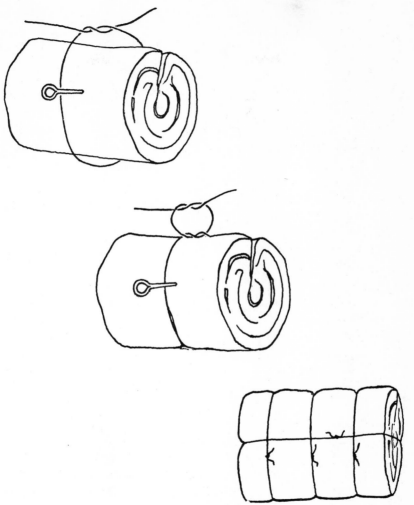

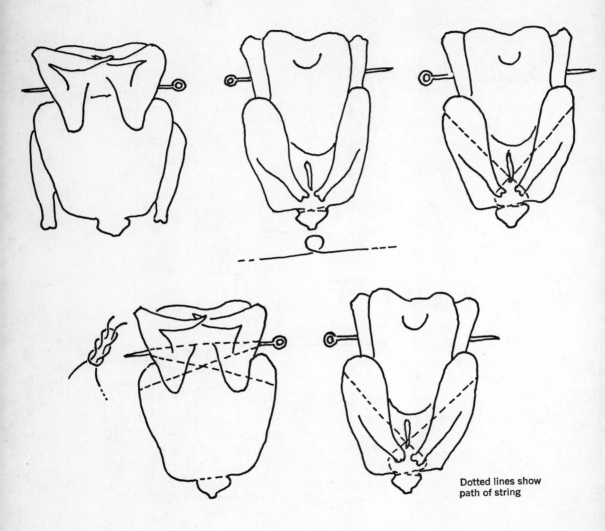

Dotted lines show
path of string

KNOT DOUBLED. Draw up as tightly as you can, and complete by making a SQUARE KNOT DOUBLED. Cut the string neatly close to the knot. Repeat the operation near one end of the roll, turn it around, and put a tie near the other end. Now fill the spaces between the *ties* with as many more as you think will be needed to hold the roast together while cooking. For most roasts ties spaced ¾″ to 1″ apart should be quite adequate. Now pass a tie right round the sides and ends of the roll and finish with a SQUARE KNOT DOUBLED. But keep this tie well away from the join in the roll—if it slips into the join the tie will become slack and useless.

A bird, whether it be a chicken, a turkey, a duck, or a goose, to be roasted in the oven or turned on the spit, should be neatly and firmly trussed beforehand, so it will hold together in the cooking.

Here is, I think, the best way to do it:

I assume the bird has been drawn and cleaned. If it has been sold as "oven ready," remove the strings with which it has been trussed.

Lay it on its breast. Tuck the wing tips behind the back on either side. Run a metal skewer through the wings, just above the elbow joints, to hold the wings in place. Turn the bird on its back. Cut a piece of string about four feet long. Middle it, but leave one leg a few inches longer than the other. Lay the middle of the string over the tailpiece and take a tight *round turn,* bringing the two legs of the string upward. Cross the two legs of string over the ends of the leg bones of the bird and below the end of the breast bone over the vent where the bird has been opened for cleaning. Now, holding the two legs of string in either hand, take the strings high up over the drumsticks where they join the second joints. Still holding the legs of string, roll the bird over on its breast again. Cross the strings over the back, just over the wing joints, and take a turn around each end of the skewer. Cross the strings again over the ends of the skewer, and pull up on either leg of the string as tightly as possible, so that the legs and wings of the bird are held firmly up against the body. Tie an OVERHAND KNOT DOUBLED near one end of the skewer. Tighten the strings once more, and tie another OVERHAND KNOT DOUBLED to make a SQUARE KNOT DOUBLED, and trim off the ends of string close to the knot.

The great advantage of this method is that when the bird comes to the table to be carved, all the carver has to do is to hold the bird firmly with his fork and then to pry out the skewer with the point of his carving knife. The string will now come away from the bird in one single long loop, without needing to be cut. No messy bits on the platter.

And if the bird has been stuffed, the crossed strings over the ends of the drumsticks will hold the vent closed and so keep the stuffing from coming out in the cooking.

There is no other method of trussing a fowl that I know of which does not involve having to cut the string in one or more places in order to remove it.

Chapter ix ▪ Stopping, Whipping, and Seizing

A *"stopping"* is a *temporary* method of preventing the strands of a laid rope or braided line or cord from unlaying beyond a certain point, or from fraying at a cut end.

A *"whipping"* is a *permanent* method of preventing the strands of a laid rope or braided line or cord from unlaying beyond a certain point, or from fraying at a cut end. The name *whipping* derives from its use on the reef points in sails, to prevent the soft cord of which the reef points were made from wearing and fraying as the wind whipped and slatted them against the canvas. Reef points were always whipped twice, once at each end and again nearer the sail. The whipping was done with a sail-maker's needle and palm.

A *"seizing"* may be either temporary or permanent, and is a method of fastening together two parts of rope or cord that lie alongside and parallel to each other so that they will not slip or slide against each other when a strain is put on one or both of them.

Stoppings and *whippings* are always made with material which is much thinner than the rope or cord to which they are being attached. For the sizes of rope or cord which will normally be encountered around the house or the farm, up to, say, two inches in cir-

115

cumference—rather less than three-quarters of an inch in diameter —the best material is probably the strong brown thread that is used by shoemakers and saddlemakers. Failing that, then the fine twine that is sold by the ball in most stationery stores. Fine fishing line is excellent, but rather expensive.

A *whipping,* which is meant to be permanent, will be much stronger and more durable if the thread or twine is well waxed beforehand. You can buy a cake of beeswax from almost any shoemaker or saddlemaker and it will last for years. It is possible to buy shoemaker's thread already waxed and put up on reels ready for use on the sewing machines used in stitching and repairing shoes. But that also is rather expensive. It is cheaper to get a ball of thread from the shoemaker and wax it yourself.

Rather heavier stuff, fairly stout twine or string, is needed for *seizings,* unless the rope or cord to be seized is quite small in size.

Stopping

The simplest way to put on a *stopping* is to take two or three *round turns* around the rope or cord with the thread, pull the turns up very tightly, and secure the thread over the turns with a SQUARE KNOT.

A stronger and neater method is to take a short piece of thread a foot or so long and start by laying a couple of inches of thread along the rope with the end leading to the right. Hold it in place under the left thumb. Bring the rest of the thread around the rope from back to front, and lead it to the right, so that it forms an *open loop* below the rope. Now take several—three or four—loose turns with the thread, but this time from front to back, around the rope *inside* the loop, working backward along the rope from right to left.

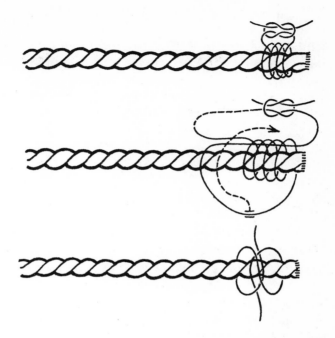

Stoppings

Now with the loop you take tight turns around the rope and the two ends of thread, working from left to right. As you make each turn, one turn will unwind from the loose turns inside the loop until you have made as many tight turns as you originally made loose ones. Now take the slack out of the loop by pulling on the end of thread leading to the left until it is tight, then do the same with the end of the thread leading to the right. When the turns are as tight as you can make them by pulling on the ends, finish off with a SQUARE KNOT over all the turns.

But the best *stopping* of all is the BAG KNOT. This can be put on and drawn up more tightly than the two given above, and so will hold the strands of rope together more firmly. If you are *stopping* the cut end of a rope to keep it from fraying, you can tie the BAG KNOT by the quick method given in Chapter III (p. 51). And if you want to be able to take your *stopping* off quickly and easily, you can use the SLIPPED BAG KNOT, whereas with the first two methods described, you will probably have to cut the *stopping* to get it off.

Whipping

A *whipping* may be put on at the cut end of a rope or line, or anywhere along its length. It may be any number of turns of the thread or twine, depending on how wide the *whipping* is to be. *Whippings* may be put on along the length of a rope at measured distances apart, as markers to show how much rope has been paid out. Or a *whipping* may be put on at a point where the rope has to pass over a hook or through an eye of some kind, and there is risk of the strands of the rope being chafed and worn. But these latter uses, ashore at any rate, will be rather unusual.

      By far the most frequent use of a *whipping* is to prevent the cut end of a rope or line from fraying.

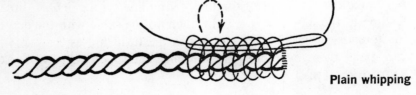

Plain whipping

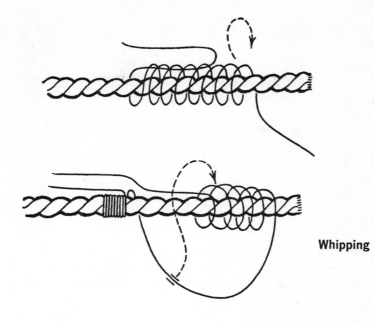

Whipping

Whipping

Before you start putting on a *whipping* you must determine the length of thread or twine you will need. The easiest way to estimate this is to remember that you will need a length of thread about four times the diameter of the rope to make each turn of the *whipping*. For example, you want to put a *whipping* on a rope about ½″ in diameter. (This will be 1½″ rope measured by its circumference.) Four times ½″ will be 2″. If you are going to put a whipping of thirteen turns, you will need 26″ of thread. As it is always better to overestimate rather than underestimate (it is very irritating to find that your piece of thread is just not *quite* long enough to complete your *whipping*), allow a few more inches and cut it three feet in length.

To make a neat job at the cut end of a rope the *whipping* should be about as wide as the diameter of the rope, so that looked at from the side, the *whipping* will appear approximately square.

Having cut off a piece of thread the right length, take the rope in your left hand near the cut end you want to whip. Turn back one end of the thread to make a *closed loop* two or three inches long and lay the loop along the rope with the eye of the loop projecting a little beyond the end of the rope. Steady the loop of thread under the left thumb. Now take tight turns with the thread around the rope and the loop, working from left to right (toward the cut end of the rope) until you have put on enough turns to make the *whipping* the desired width—approximately the diameter of the rope.

Now pass the end of the thread with which you have been making the turns through the eye of the loop. Holding the cut end of the rope and the *whipping* firmly by the thumb and fingers of the right hand, with the left hand pull gently on the end of the thread leading from under the *whipping* to the left—that is, the end with which you made the initial loop. As you pull on this end, the other

end will be drawn under the *whipping* by the loop. When you can
see, or guess, that you have drawn enough to bring the crossing of
the threads under the middle of the *whipping,* start pulling gently on
both ends of the thread equally, to tighten the outside turns of the
whipping. When the whole *whipping* is taut and firm, snip off the
loose ends of thread as close to the *whipping* as possible.

After the *whipping* is completed, you should either pound it all
around with a mallet or a piece of wood to smooth it, or roll it between two pieces of wood. And there's no law against your rolling it
between the sole of your shoe and the floor.

This makes a very neat and tidy *whipping,* but it is not a very
strong or durable one if the end of the rope is to get much rough
treatment.

The following *whipping* is not as neat, because it leaves a knot
showing, but is not only more durable but rather quicker and easier
to put on.

First I want to describe the way you would do it if you were
putting on your *whipping* somewhere along the length of the rope,
not at an end. Lay one end of your piece of thread along the rope
from left to right, and hold it under your left thumb. With the right
hand take, say, five tight turns of the thread around the rope and
end of thread, working from left to right. Then lay the end of the
thread lying along the rope back to the left over the turns. Take
three more turns. Now, pinning the turns you have already put on
under the left thumb, lead the *free end* of the thread to the right,
leaving a loop under the rope, pass it over the rope from front to
back, and then make five loose turns around the rope *inside* the
loop, working from right to left. Lay the *free end* of the thread over
the turns already made, and with the slack in the loop continue
making the turns of the whipping, from left to right. As you make

each turn a turn will unwind from the right end of the loop. When you have put on five turns, change hands, and hold down the turns of the *whipping* with the right thumb. With the left hand pull the *free end* to the left until all the slack in the loop has been taken up, and the right end of the *whipping* is tight and firm. Do the same with the other end of thread to make the left end firm. Finish off with a SQUARE KNOT over the three center turns, and pound or roll the *whipping* as previously described.

If you are putting this *whipping* on the cut end of a rope, you need not bother to make the loop and put the turns on inside it as above. When you have put on the three center turns, simply lay the *free end* back from right to left over the turns and hold with the left thumb. Now you can continue putting on the turns merely by giving the loop a twist each time it has to pass over the end of the rope, until you have put on the remaining five turns. Then draw the ends up and finish with a SQUARE KNOT as above.

I have cited the 5—3—5 *whipping* because thirteen turns will usually be adequate for most sizes of rope likely to be encountered ashore. But on the smaller sizes 4—2—4 may be enough, and on the larger sizes you may want to do 7—4—7, or a total of eighteen turns. A little practice will enable you to estimate how wide your *whipping* needs to be, and how many turns will be required.

There may not be frequent occasion to use *whipping* in the average household, though it seems to me that, for appearance's sake if for no other reason, all braided clothesline, Venetian blind cords, curtain pulls, and suchlike should be whipped. Certainly in the garage, on the farm, in the workshop, wherever rope is in use, the cut ends should always be whipped.

And once the principle is learned, there are all sorts of uses to which *whipping* can be put. Let me give just one example of its possible use in the kitchen. If you have a frying pan or a saucepan or a coffee pot with a metal handle that gets too hot to hold without a pot-holder, quite the best way to insulate it is by putting on a *whipping* of Venetian blind cord or some similar material of appropriate size the whole length of the handle. When the *whipping* is completed, take a tube of one of the clear glues you can buy in any stationery store or hardware store, spread glue fairly thickly all over the *whipping,* rub it well into the cord with the tip of your little finger, and let it dry well for 24 or 48 hours. Then give the *whipping* two coats of enamel paint of your favourite kitchen colour, and you'll never need to use a pot-holder again for that utensil—or burn yourself if you forget and try to pick it up without the potholder.

Seizing

Seizing again is something that perhaps may not be frequently used in the average household. But it is a method which everyone who occasionally has to use rope or cord should know. It is altogether the best way of making completely secure a knot that is going to be left permanently in the rope or cord in which it has been tied, to prevent the knot from loosening or becoming deformed.

Though *seizing* has many other uses, especially aboard ship, it is the one above that I am going to cite as illustration. Say you are going to leave a rope or cord permanently attached to a ring on a wall, and you have chosen a ROUND TURN and TWO HALF HITCHES as the most suitable knot to attach the rope to the ring.

Having finished the knot, cut a good length of stout twine or string—you'll probably need six to seven feet if the rope is ½″ in diameter. Lay the *working end* of the rope which comes out of the

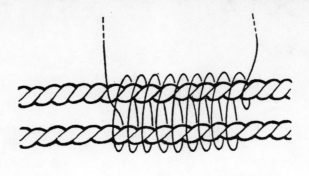

Seizing

second HALF HITCH close alongside the *working part*. Leaving about a foot of the *working end* of the twine loose, take ten or twelve tight turns around both parts of the rope. Then, working backward, put another layer of turns on top of the first layer. You must make the first layer of turns as tight as possible; the second layer can be a little looser.

Pass the *working end* of the twine up between the two parts of the rope, take it across the turns, down between the two parts of the rope and back across the turns on the opposite side. Repeat once more, so that you have two full turns of the *working end* around the two layers of turns on the rope. Do the same with the *free end* of the twine, but take it across the turns in the opposite direction from the *working end,* so that when you have passed it around the turns twice, the two ends will meet in the middle of the *seizing*. Draw both ends up very tightly, so that the two layers of turns are compressed against the two parts of the rope.

Finish by tying a SQUARE KNOT with the two ends, and snip off any surplus twine.

The *seizing* above is very secure if made over two parts of the same rope, or two pieces of rope of the same size. However, if you should have to seize two pieces of rope of different sizes, one larger, one smaller, a slightly different technique is advisable. Instead of taking the turns of the twine right round the ropes, put on what are called *"racking"* turns. These are made by passing the twine between the two ropes alternately from front to back and from back to front on each turn, so that the twine forms a series of figure 8's around the two ropes. With this method you only put on one layer of turns instead of two, but more of them, say fifteen to twenty instead of ten or twelve. The *seizing* is then finished off as the one above, by taking the two ends of twine around the turns and between the two ropes in opposite directions twice, and securing with a SQUARE KNOT.

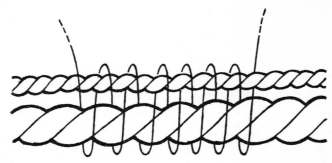

Racking turns

Index

(Note: Page numbers given below refer to the page in the text on which the first full description or definition of the knot, word or phrase appears.)